Business English

Basic Communication Skills
for International Business Situations

Kazushige Tsuji   Setsu Tsuji   Margaret M. Li

Asahi Press

音声再生アプリ「リスニング・トレーナー」を使った音声ダウンロード

朝日出版社開発のアプリ、「リスニング・トレーナー（リストレ）」を使えば、教科書の音声をスマホ、タブレットに簡単にダウンロードできます。どうぞご活用ください。

◉ アプリ【リスニング・トレーナー】の使い方

《アプリのダウンロード》

App Store または Google Play から「リスニング・トレーナー」のアプリ（無料）をダウンロード

App Storeはこちら▶ 　　Google Playはこちら▶

《アプリの使い方》

① アプリを開き「コンテンツを追加」をタップ
② 画面上部に【15659】を入力しDoneをタップ

音声ストリーミング配信 ⟩⟩⟩

この教科書の音声は、右記ウェブサイトにて無料で配信しています。

https://text.asahipress.com/free/english/

はじめに

　グローバル化時代と言われて久しいですが、世界は新たにWith/Postコロナの時代に突入し、企業のグローバル経営も新しい局面を迎えています。このように目まぐるしく状況が変わる時代において、国際ビジネスにおける英語対応能力はさらに必要性を増しており、「実践ビジネス英語」の力を身につけることでキャリア形成の幅を広げることができる時代だとも言えます。将来グローバル企業に勤めたい、あるいは海外と関わりのある仕事がしたい学生のみなさんのために本書を作成しました。

　内容は、大学生の主人公が就職活動を経て東京に本社のあるElec International Corporationに就職し、米国のEco Motors Inc.との電気自動車開発を目指す国際プロジェクトに携るというストーリー展開になっています。国際的な職場環境で必要とされる英語コミュニケーション力を養うと同時に、国際業務の基本的な流れを学べるように工夫してあります。

　本書には各種ビジネスシーンを取り上げた12のユニットがあり、各ユニットはPart 1とPart 2から構成されています。Part 1ではオフィスでのコミュニケーションの基礎を、Part 2では電話でのコミュニケーションの基礎を学習します。最後のBusiness Topic（英語）とBusiness Tips（日本語）では、各ユニットに関連したテーマを取り上げており、国際ビジネスの実用的な知識を身につけることができます。

　『Business English』で学んだことを活かし、みなさんが将来の職場で活躍されることを願ってやみません。

著者 ｜ 辻 和成
　　　辻 勢都
　｜ Margaret M. Lieb

C O N T E N T S

本 書 の 特 徴

　本書の各ユニットは、Part 1の「In Person」、Part2の「Telephone Communication」、そして「Business Topic」から構成されています。

　Part 1とPart 2は、ユニットが進むにつれてストーリーが展開されます。また、「Business Topic」は、各ユニットのテーマにそった内容になっています。各ユニットのPart1とPart 2の最初にはシーンの説明があるので、学ぶべきターゲットが明確にわかり、学習しやすくなっています。

　授業では、本書を最初からページ順に進める以外にも、目的に応じてPart1、Part2、Business Topicをそれぞれを独立したユニットとして使用することもできます。

各ユニットの構成

Part 1　In Person

1 **Vocabulary Building**
   ▶ダイアログの重要語句を学ぶ。

2 **Listening（1）**
   ▶ダイアログを聞いて内容を把握する。
   ▶設問の答えを選択する。

3 **Listening（2）**
   ▶ダイアログを聞いて空欄を埋める。
   ▶リピート練習を行う。

4 **Role Play**
   ▶ダイアログのロールプレイ練習を行う。

5 **Reading &Writing**
   ▶各種ビジネス文書の内容を読み取る。
   ▶情報を記入し、ビジネス文書を完成させる。

Part 2　Telephone Communication

1 **Listening（1）**
   ▶ダイアログを聞いて内容を把握する。
   ▶正誤問題を解く。

2 **Listening（2）**
   ▶ダイアログを聞いて空欄を埋める。
   ▶リピート練習を行う。

3 **Role Play**
   ▶ダイアログのロールプレイ練習を行う。

4 **Conversation Map**
   ▶フローに従って電話会話を完成させる。
   ▶ペア練習を行う。

Business Topic

各ユニットに関連したテーマを取り扱ったBusiness Topic（英語）の読解問題。
また、Business Tips（日本語）で、国際ビジネスの実用的知識を深める。

 音声が用意されており、リピーティングおよびシャドーイング練習ができる。

Business English

本書に登場する企業とおもな人物

Elec International Corporation （エレックインターナショナル株式会社）

東京に本社がある企業。電気自動車やハイブリッド車用の部品・コンポーネントの開発を行っている。

 谷 明
[社長]

 Jack Fenton
[人事部 部長]

 Cindy Larson
[人事部 スタッフ]

 Charles Rock
[国際営業部 部長]

 田川真理子
[国際営業部 課長]

 木村良太（主人公）
[国際営業部 スタッフ]

 岡 弘
[EVコンポーネント開発部 部長]

 井関太郎
[湘南工場生産部門 常務]

Eco Motors Inc.

アメリカ企業で電気自動車を製造・販売しているメーカー。エレックインターナショナル株式会社の大株主である。

 Tom Davis
[Director, Engineering Division]

 Mary Smith
[Engineer]
※Elec International 社に赴任中

 Tony Dickinson
[Manager, International Purchasing Department]

 Ann Roberts
[Engineer, EV Testing & Research Department]

その他

さくら大学

 Mike
[木村良太の大学時代の英語教員]

Unit 1　Job Hunting　就職活動

Part 1　In Person

SCENE

国際プロジェクトに携わるチャンスがある仕事に就くことを希望している木村良太は、就職活動について、外国人の英語教師に相談しています。

1 ▸ Vocabulary Building

[1] 次の英語の語句を聞いて日本語の意味と結び付けなさい。

[2] もう一度英語の語句を聞いてそれぞれ発音しなさい。

regarding ●	● 外資系企業
participate in ●	● 業界
project ●	● ～に関して
industry ●	● ～に参加する
potential ●	● 事業
foreign affiliated company ●	● 可能性

2 ▸ Listening（1）

良太と英語教師Mikeのダイアログを聞いて、各設問に対するもっとも適切な答えを選びなさい。

1　**What kind of job is Ryota interested in?**

    A　A job which requires him to improve his English.

    B　A job which allows him to work internationally.

    C　A job which allows him to travel overseas.

    D　A job which requires him to work domestically.

2　**How can Ryota get information about possible jobs?**

    A　He can ask other teachers.

    B　He can randomly call companies.

    C　He can use his cellphone.

    D　He can visit the career center.

3 ▶ Listening(2)

もう一度ダイアログを聞きながら空欄を埋めなさい。
ダイアログが完成したらリピート練習をしなさい。

Ryota: Excuse me, ①_____ ?

Mike: Sure. What can I do for you?

Ryota: I would like to ask your advice regarding job hunting.

Mike: What kind of job are you looking for?

Ryota: I'd like a job which ②_____ international projects.

Mike: OK. Is there any particular industry ③_____ ?

Ryota: I value ④_____ more than a particular type of industry.

Mike: Do you have any specific company in mind?

Ryota: Not really. If there is ⑤_____ working internationally, I am willing to ⑥_____ .

Mike: Well, first, ⑦_____ foreign affiliated companies?

Ryota: That's a good idea. How can I find out about them?

Mike: Well, ⑧_____ , you could ⑨_____ our career center.

Ryota: I see, and I can ⑩_____ , too. Thank you very much.

Mike: You are most welcome.

4 ▶ Role Play

完成したダイアログを使ってロールプレイ練習をしなさい。

5 ▶ Reading &Writing

[1] 次の求人広告を読んで質問に答えなさい。

> **Sales & marketing** staff for electronic vehicle parts and components manufacturer. All nationalities welcome. Good communication skills in Japanese & English. PC skills required. Excellent working conditions with international travel opportunities and perks. Send resume to Jack Fenton, General Manager, Personnel Dept., Elec International Inc., World Tower Bldg. 28th Floor, 1-2, Roppongi, Minato-ku, Tokyo 106-0032. Call 03-3486-11××for details.

〈 1 〉 どんな会社がどんな人材を求めていますか？
〈 2 〉 応募者の必要条件は何ですか？
〈 3 〉 応募するにはどうすればよいですか？
〈 4 〉 Jack Fentonの肩書と所属部署は何ですか？

[2] 以下は[1]の求人に応募するための手紙です。

〈**1**〉 下のA～Fの語句を使って空欄を埋めなさい。

〈**2**〉 〔a〕～〔d〕の4つの段落を並べ替えて手紙を完成させなさい。

1 - 3 Tsubaki-cho, 1- chome
Setagaya-ku, Tokyo 158 - 7630

January 23, 20××

Mr. Jack Fenton, General Manager
Personnel Department
Elec International Corporation.
World Tower Bldg., 28th Floor
1-2 Roppongi, Minato-ku
Tokyo 106-0032

Dear Mr. Fenton:

〔a〕 I have also worked hard on my English. In addition to studying Business English in college, I was also an ① _____ student at Griffith State University in the U.S. for four months. Thus, I believe that I am now ② _____ for the position you are

③ _____ .

〔b〕 I would greatly appreciate your granting me an interview. I can be reached any time at 090 - 9102 - 57××.

〔c〕 I saw the advertisement on your website for a sales and marketing position. I would like to apply for this position, and am enclosing my resume.

〔d〕 I will be graduating from Sakura University in March next year with a ④ _____ degree in ⑤ _____ . I have taken such courses as   International Management and Intercultural Communication which I feel prepare me for work in sales and marketing.

Sincerely yours,

Ryota Kimura
Ryota Kimura

Encl: ⑥ _____

A	resume	D	offering
B	exchange	E	business administration
C	qualified	F	bachelor's

※**必要事項をコンパクトに**：応募の手紙には、求人を知った方法、応募する職種、応募の理由、自分をアピールする要素、面接の希望、自分の連絡先などを要領よく書きます。

Part 2 Telephone Communication

SCENE

木村良太は、希望する職場のひとつであるElec International
社に電話をかけて、面接の詳細を聞こうとしています。ここでは、
電話を「取り次いでもらう」および「取り次ぐ」場合のコミュニケー
ションのしかたがポイントになります。

1 ▶ Listening (1)

良太の電話をElec International社の社員が取り次いでいます。ダイアログを聞いて、次の各文の内容が正しければTを、
間違っていればFを選びなさい。

1　Ryota wants to talk to Mr. Fenton in the Sales Department.　　T / F
2　Ryota is calling to enquire about the job opening.　　T / F
3　Mr. Fenton is not available.　　T / F

2 ▶ Listening (2)

もう一度ダイアログを聞きながら空欄を埋めなさい。ダイアログが完成したらリピート練習をしなさい。

Cindy: Personnel Department, Cindy Larson speaking. ①＿＿＿＿＿＿＿＿＿＿＿?
Ryota: Yes, could I speak to Mr. Jack Fenton, please?
Cindy: Sure, may I ask ②＿＿＿＿＿＿＿＿＿?(*1)
Ryota: ③＿＿＿＿＿＿＿＿ Ryota Kimura, and I'm calling about the position
　　　④＿＿＿＿＿＿＿＿＿.
Cindy: OK, thank you, Mr. Kimura. Could you please ⑤＿＿＿＿＿＿＿＿ you?
Ryota: Yes, thank you.
Cindy: One moment, please. (*2) (*To Mr. Fenton*) Mr. Fenton, a Mr. Kimura is
　　　⑥＿＿＿＿＿＿＿＿＿ enquiring about our online job ad.
Fenton: OK, you can go ahead and ⑦＿＿＿＿＿＿＿.(*3)
Cindy: Certainly. (*To Ryota*) ⑧＿＿＿＿＿＿＿＿＿, please.
Fenton: This is Jack Fenton. Can I help you, Mr. Kimura?
Ryota: Yes, I'm interested in the job advertised on your website....

Notes　*1　相手を確かめる表現。ほかにMay I ask your name? / Could I have your name, please?など。名前が聞き取れなかったときは
　　　　I'm sorry, but I didn't catch your name.、名前のスペルを聞くときはCould you spell your name, please?など。
　　　　*2　取り次ぎで相手を待たせるときの表現。Hold on. / One moment. / Just a moment. / Just a second.など。
　　　　*3　connect ... with ～ も「…を～につなぐ」、transfer ... to ～ は「…を～に回す」。

3 ▶ Role Play

完成したダイアログを使ってロールプレイ練習をしなさい。

4 ▶ Conversation Map

それぞれの英語のせりふを考えて、電話でのコミュニケーションを成立させなさい。完成したらペアで会話しなさい。

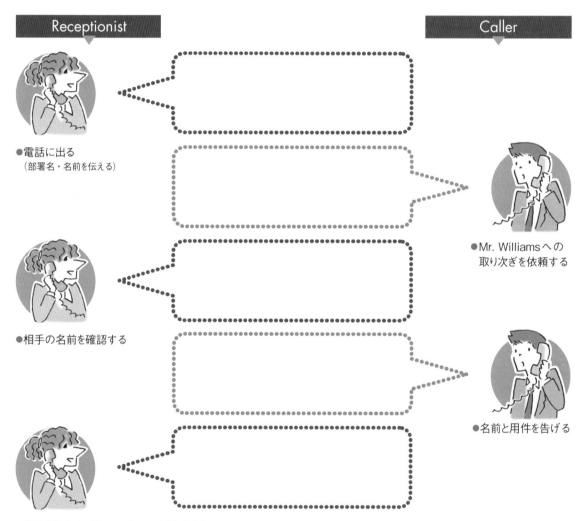

Receptionist

●電話に出る
（部署名・名前を伝える）

●相手の名前を確認する

●相手を待たせてMr. Williamsを呼び出す
●Mr. Williamsに伝え、取り次ぐように言われる
●了解して相手に取り次ぐ

Caller

●Mr. Williamsへの
　取り次ぎを依頼する

●名前と用件を告げる

Business Topic ▶ ❶

高まるビジネス英語の必要性

1 次の英文から、「日本の職場において英語が使用されるようになってきた理由」を読み取りなさい。

2 音声を聞きながらシャドーイングの練習をしなさい。

The Increasing Demand for English Proficiency at Work

Currently English is widespread in international business. In the past, a limited number of people used English in their jobs in Japan. However, because of globalization, more and more Japanese companies are facing the prospect of conducting communication in English. For example, employees of many companies are provided with computers and exchange emails in English with their counterparts overseas. What is more, video conferences are increasingly being held between Japanese and foreign companies more often than ever thanks to the rapid advancement of ICT*. Under such circumstances, proficiency in English has become increasingly important at many workplaces going global and is often necessary for promotion.

* ICT: Information and Communication Technology の略で、通信技術を活用したコミュニケーションを指す。

Business Tips

英語力とキャリア

かつて英語を必要とする職場は、特定の業界や会社、あるいは一定の部署でした。しかし今日では、英語を必要とする職場が急速に増えています。また、昇進や昇格の要件として一定の英語力を求めたり、採用時に英語力を評価したりする企業も増えています。さらに、事業のグローバル化展開を進める企業では、社員教育の一環として英語研修を実施しているところもあります。すなわち、ビジネス英語力をつければ、キャリアの選択肢が広がる時代だと言えるのです。

Unit 2 Job Interviews 面接

Part 1 In Person

SCENE

今日はいよいよ良太の面接日です。良太が就職を希望する外資系企業Elec International社が募集しているのは、英語が堪能な営業担当です。採用担当である人事部のJack Fenton部長との英語面接が進められています。

1 ▶ Vocabulary Building

[1] 次の英語の語句を聞いて日本語の意味と結び付けなさい。

[2] もう一度英語の語句を聞いてそれぞれ発音しなさい。

strength ●   ● 達成感

cooperative ●   ● 協力的な

persistent ●   ● 目的追求的な

a sense of fulfillment ●   ● 強み

goal-oriented ●   ● 技量

proficiency ●   ● ねばり強い

2 ▶ Listening（1）

面接における良太とJack Fenton部長のダイアログを聞いて、各設問に対するもっとも適切な答えを選びなさい。

1 **What does Ryota want to do in his job?**

　　A He wants to live abroad.

　　B He wants to work on international projects.

　　C He wants to travel to the US.

　　D He wants to meet people from other countries.

2 **What is necessary to succeed in this company?**

　　A Dependency.

　　B Consistency.

　　C Clear goals.

　　D A good command of Japanese.

3 ▶ Listening（2）

14

もう一度ダイアログを聞きながら空欄を埋めなさい。
ダイアログが完成したらリピート練習をしなさい。

Jack: ①＿＿＿＿＿＿＿＿＿＿ about this job?

Ryota: My career goal is to work internationally. I believe this job would give me the opportunity to do that.

Jack: OK. So, what would you like to be doing in five years?

Ryota: I'd like to ②＿＿＿＿＿＿＿＿＿＿ international projects.

Jack: I see. So, what are your strengths?

Ryota: I do my best to be ③＿＿＿＿＿＿＿＿＿＿.

Jack: And what do you look for in a job?

Ryota: I look for opportunities to ④＿＿＿＿＿＿＿＿＿. I need to have ⑤＿＿＿＿＿＿＿＿.

Jack: OK, that's about all from us. Do you have any questions?

Ryota: Yes, I wanted to ask you ⑥＿＿＿＿＿＿＿＿＿＿ in this job?

Jack: Well, you need to be ⑦＿＿＿＿＿＿＿＿＿. Also, English proficiency is essential.

Ryota: I see. I'll work hard to ⑧＿＿＿＿＿＿＿＿＿, if I am offered the job.

Jack: Mr. Kimura, thank you for coming today. We'll be ⑨＿＿＿＿＿＿＿＿＿ you soon.

Ryota: Thank you for your time, Mr. Fenton.

4 ▶ Role Play

完成したダイアログを使ってロールプレイ練習をしなさい。

5 ▶ Reading &Writing

[1] 次のページに木村良太の履歴書があります。A〜Iの語句を使って空欄を埋め、履歴書を完成させなさい。

[2] 木村良太の学歴・職歴・資格・趣味を説明しなさい。

RYOTA KIMURA

Address: 1-1-3, Tsubaki-cho, Setagaya-ku, Tokyo 158-7630
Mobile: 090-9102-57××
E-mail: ryota55@stj.ne.jp

(①):   A (②) in international sales and marketing

Date of Birth: July 5, 19××

EDUCATION:
20××- present   Sakura University, Tokyo

                       Expected graduation date: March 20××

                       (③):(④) of Business Administration

                       Major courses included International Management,

                       Intercultural Communication, and Business English

Spring Term 20××   Griffith State University, San Francisco, California

                       4-month English course as an (⑤)

20××- 20××   Hyogo Prefectural Aoyama High School, Nishinomiya

                       Treasurer of Student Council, 20××- 20××

WORK EXPERIENCE:
20××- present   Part-time instructor at Ken Juku, a cram school, Tokyo

                       Responsible for teaching English and mathematics

(⑥):   (⑦):TOEIC 820, STEP, Pre-1st grade

                       Bookkeeping:Nissho 2nd grade

                       Computer skills:Word, Excel and PowerPoint

INTERESTS: Traveling and listening to music

(⑧):   Available upon request

※現在では、Age and Gender（年齢・性別）、Marital status（婚姻関係の有無）は書かない。

A	references	E	objective
B	English proficiency	F	position
C	exchange student	G	qualifications
D	degree	H	bachelor

Part 2 Telephone Communication

SCENE

Elec International社の田川真理子が外部からかかってきた電話に出て応対していますが、相手が話したい人物が社には存在しません。ここでは、「**間違い電話がかかってきたときのコミュニケーション**」のしかたがポイントになります。

1 ▶ Listening (1)

田川真理子の電話応対のダイアログを聞いて、次の各文が正しければTを、間違っていればFを選びなさい。

1 The caller works for NBC Corporation.   T / F
2 The caller wants to talk to Mr. James Parker.   T / F
3 The caller dialed the wrong number.   T / F

2 ▶ Listening (2)

もう一度ダイアログを聞きながら空欄を埋めなさい。ダイアログが完成したらリピート練習をしなさい。

Caller: Could I speak to Mr. Parker, please?

Mariko: Sure, ①_____ who's calling, please?

Caller: This is Peter Rix of NBC Corporation.

Mariko: Thank you, Mr. Rix. Actually, ②_____ Mr. Parkers here, James
　　　　Parker and Robert Parker.(*1)

Caller: Oh, isn't there a Mr. Jason Parker there?

Mariko: No, ③_____ there is no one here ④_____.(*2)

Caller: Oh really? That's strange.

Mariko: Well, let's see. ⑤_____ did you call?

Caller: 03-3456- ⑥_____.

Mariko: Ah, that's why. Looks like you've got ⑦_____.(*3) This is 3456-
　　　　⑧_____.

Caller: Oh, really? Sorry about that.

Mariko: That's quite all right. Bye now.

Caller: Thank you. Bye.

Notes　*1　同じ名字の者がいる場合の表現。
　　　　　*2　相手が求めている名前の人物が存在しないことを伝える表現。
　　　　　*3　間違い電話であることを告げる表現。

3 ▶ Role Play

完成したダイアログを使ってロールプレイ練習をしなさい。

4 ▶ Conversation Map

それぞれの英語のせりふを考えて、電話でのコミュニケーションを成立させなさい。完成したらペアで会話しなさい。

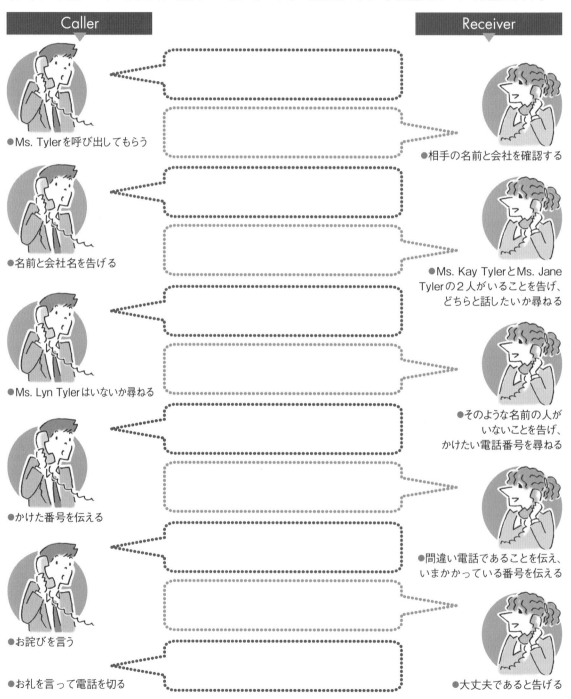

Caller	Receiver
●Ms. Tylerを呼び出してもらう	●相手の名前と会社を確認する
●名前と会社名を告げる	●Ms. Kay TylerとMs. Jane Tylerの2人がいることを告げ、どちらと話したいか尋ねる
●Ms. Lyn Tylerはいないか尋ねる	●そのような名前の人がいないことを告げ、かけたい電話番号を尋ねる
●かけた番号を伝える	●間違い電話であることを伝え、いまかかっている番号を伝える
●お詫びを言う	●大丈夫であると告げる
●お礼を言って電話を切る	

Business Topic ▶ ❷

就職面接のポイント

1 次の英文から、「就職面接の際、事前に準備すべきこと、面接中に注意すべき点」を読み取りなさい。。

2 音声を聞きながらリピーティングとシャドーイングの練習をしなさい。

Tips for Successful Job Interviews

A successful interview requires thorough preparation. First, it is essential to fully understand what the job involves. For this reason, you should research the company with which you are seeking the position. In addition, you should be ready to explain your strengths and weaknesses. You should also be aware that the first impression is very important. Thus, you need to strive to convey confidence and professionalism. Maintain good posture, keep your back straight and pay attention to how you speak. Volume, speed and intonation are also key to a successful interview. Moreover, eye contact plays an important role in making a good first impression. You must also listen carefully to the interviewers' questions, try to answer them clearly, and keep to the point.

Business Tips

グローバル経営を展開する企業が求める人材とは?

グローバル人材に必要な要素として、文部科学省は「グローバル人材育成推進会議中間まとめ」（2011）の中で以下のような項目を挙げています。
- 語学力・コミュニケーション能力
- 主体性・積極性、チャレンジ精神、協調性・柔軟性、責任感・使命感
- 異文化に対する理解と、日本人としてのアイデンティティー

企業は今、国内市場の縮小傾向を受け、経済成長が見込まれる海外市場を目指しています。同時に会社組織の多国籍化が進んでいます。その結果、さまざまな国籍、習慣、価値観が混在するチームを束ね、課題を解決して成果に結びつける力を備えたグローバル人材が必要となります。

Unit 3 Company Profile 会社プロフィール

Part 1 In Person

SCENE

良太は、グローバルに事業展開を行っている企業Elec International社に内定が決まりました。さっそく就職の相談をしたさくら大学のMike先生に、どのような会社から内定をもらったのか報告します。

1 ▶ Vocabulary Building

[1] 次の英語の語句を聞いて日本語の意味と結び付けなさい。

[2] もう一度英語の語句を聞いてそれぞれ発音しなさい。

employment ●　　　● 年間売上
manufacturer ●　　　● 工場
global warming ●　　　● 業績がよい
headquartered ●　　　● 本社を構えている
plant ●　　　● 地球温暖化
perform well ●　　　● 製造会社
annual sales ●　　　● 雇用

2 ▶ Listening（1）

良太とMike先生のダイアログを聞いて、各設問に対するもっとも適切な答えを選びなさい。

1　**What kind of company is Elec International?**

　A　A domestic sales company.
　B　A components supplier.
　C　An international logistics company.
　D　An electrical appliance manufacturer.

2　**What is the main advantage of an EV?**

　A　It emits carbon dioxide.
　B　It produces only a small amount of gas.
　C　It does not cause air pollution.
　D　It accelerates global warming.

3 ▶ Listening (2)

もう一度ダイアログを聞きながら空欄を埋めなさい。
ダイアログが完成したらリピート練習をしなさい。

Ryota: I have received ①_____ (*1) employment.

Mike: Congratulations! What company will you be working for?

Ryota: I'll be working for Elec International, a manufacturer of ②_____ .

Mike: Great! EVs (*2) have been ③_____ worldwide recently.

Ryota: That's right. Because of global warming, people are showing more interest in
　　　　④_____ (*3) products.

Mike: That's true. EVs don't produce any CO_2 (*4). Where ⑤_____ ?

Ryota: The company ⑥_____ in Tokyo and has a plant in Shonan.

Mike: I see. I guess the company is ⑦_____ .

Ryota: Their annual sales are approximately ⑧_____ .

Mike: Wow, that's great. I'm glad you got a good job.

Notes　*1　a notice of my employmentとも言う。
　　　　*2　EV: electric vehicle「電気自動車」の略。
　　　　*3　ecologically friendly、eco-friendly「生態学的(環境)にやさしい」とも言える。
　　　　*4　carbon dioxide「二酸化炭素」。

4 ▶ Role Play

完成したダイアログを使ってロールプレイ練習をしなさい。

5 ▶ Reading &Writing

[1] 日本語の会社プロフィールを参考に、下のA〜Hの語句を使って英語の会社プロフィールの空欄を埋めなさい。

[2] 55億と990億を英語にしてそれぞれの【　】に入れなさい。

エレックインターナショナル株式会社のプロフィール

会社名	エレックインターナショナル株式会社
社長兼最高経営責任者	谷 明
本社	〒106-0032 東京都港区六本木1丁目2番地 ワールドタワービルディング28階
設立	2001年10月5日
資本金	55億円
事業内容	電気自動車及びハイブリッド車*の部品とコンポーネントの開発、製造、販売
従業員数	1,100人（連結）
売上高	990億円（連結20××年度）
主な株主	エレックグループ会社58%、エコモーター社39%、ムーン銀行3%
子会社及び関連会社	連結子会社数4社、関連会社2社

* ハイブリッド車（hybrid vehicle）：複数の動力源を組み合わせた車。たとえばガソリンエンジンと電気モーター。

Corporate Profile of Elec International Corporation.

Company Name	Elec International Corporation
President and (①)	Akira Tani
(②)	World Tower Bldg. 28th Floor, 1-2 Roppongi, Minato-ku, Tokyo 106-0032, Japan
Established	October 5, 2001
(③)	JPY【　　　　】
Outline of Business	(④), manufacturing, and sales of hybrid and electric vehicles' parts and components
Number of (⑤)	1,100(consolidated)
Net Sales	JPY【　　　　】 (in FY 20××, consolidated)
Major (⑥)	Elec Group (58%), Eco Motors Inc.(39%), Moon Bank(3%)
(⑦) and (⑧)	4 consolidated (⑦), 2 (⑧)

A	engineering	E	capital
B	head office	F	employees
C	subsidiaries	G	affiliates
D	CEO	H	shareholders

Part 2 Telephone Communication

SCENE

Elec International社・人事部のCindy Larsonが応対した電話は、本人が不在で取り次ぐことができません。ここでは、**「電話がかかってきた本人が不在であるときのコミュニケーション」**のしかたがポイントになります。

1 ▶ Listening (1)

Cindyの電話対応のダイアログを聞いて、次の各文が正しければTを、間違っていればFを選びなさい。

1 Mr. Jack Fenton is now on vacation overseas.　　　　T / F
2 Cindy is taking a message from Mr. Shimoda.　　　　T / F
3 Mr. Shimoda wants Mr. Fenton to return his call.　　　T / F

2 ▶ Listening (2)

もう一度ダイアログを聞きながら空欄を埋めなさい。ダイアログが完成したらリピート練習をしなさい。

Cindy: Personnel Department, Cindy Larson speaking, may I help you?

Caller: Yes, may I speak to Mr. Jack Fenton, please? This is Masao Shimoda.
　　　　I ①＿＿＿＿＿＿＿＿＿＿＿Taya Machinery.

Cindy: Well, I'm afraid Mr. Fenton is ②＿＿＿＿＿＿＿＿＿ (*1) at the moment.

Caller: Oh, really? When ③＿＿＿＿＿＿＿＿ he'll be back?

Cindy: Let me see…. He's actually in the US now and ④＿＿＿＿＿＿＿＿＿ our office on
　　　　Friday of next week.

Caller: Really? ⑤＿＿＿＿＿＿＿＿ I can't talk to him sooner.

Cindy: Would you like to ⑥＿＿＿＿＿＿＿ (*2) for him?

Caller: No, that's OK. I'll try to catch him again. Thanks anyway.

Cindy: OK, then. Thank you ⑦＿＿＿＿＿＿＿＿, Mr. Shimoda. Good-bye.

Caller: Bye now.

Notes　*1　ほかに、〜 is on a business trip（出張中です）、〜 is on another line（ほかの電話に出ております）、〜 is in a meeting（会議中です）、〜 is not in the office（部署内におりません）、〜 is not at his / her desk（席を外しております）、〜 is occupied / tied up with〜（〜で手が放せません）などがある。
　　　*2　「伝言を残す」の表現。「伝言を承りましょうか」は、Shall I take a message?と聞く。

3 ▸ Role Play

完成したダイアログを使ってロールプレイ練習をしなさい。

4 ▸ Conversation Map

それぞれの英語のせりふを考えて、電話でのコミュニケーションを成立させなさい。完成したらペアで会話しなさい。

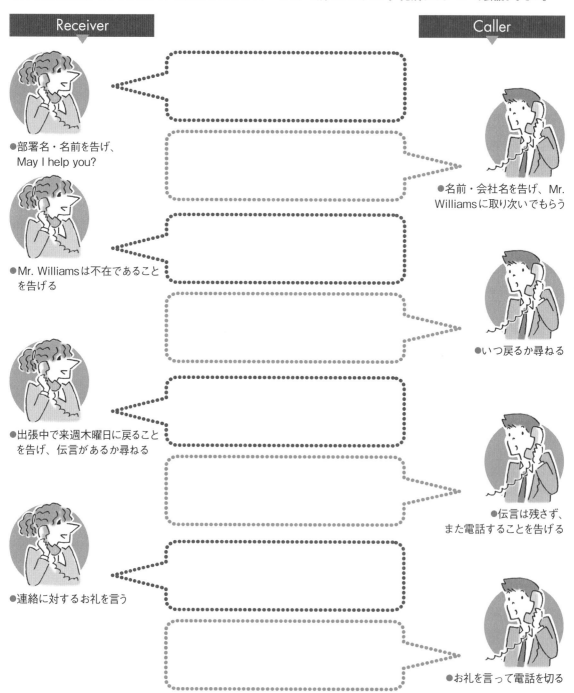

Receiver

●部署名・名前を告げ、
May I help you?

●Mr. Williamsは不在であること
を告げる

●出張中で来週木曜日に戻ること
を告げ、伝言があるか尋ねる

●連絡に対するお礼を言う

Caller

●名前・会社名を告げ、Mr.
Williamsに取り次いでもらう

●いつ戻るか尋ねる

●伝言は残さず、
また電話することを告げる

●お礼を言って電話を切る

Business Topic ▶ ❸

日本企業の特徴

1 次の英文から、「典型的な日本企業の特徴がどのように変わってきているのか、またその理由」を読み取りなさい。

2 音声を聞きながらリピーティングとシャドーイングの練習をしなさい。

Features of Japanese Companies*

Japanese companies have, until recently, often been characterized by lifetime employment. However, economic activity is now being hit hard by the spread of the new coronavirus infection worldwide, resulting in a prolonged and stagnant business climate. With a view to weathering the crisis, a large number of Japanese companies have been forced to dismiss their employees. Thus, a rising number of Japanese companies are changing their employment practices in order to stay competitive in the world market. At the same time, these companies are limiting new hires to ensure their survival. Such being the case, as a countermeasure, telework is increasingly being practiced in many companies. This trend will most likely accelerate in the workplace in line with the recent improvement in ICT.

*従来の日本型雇用システムは「三種の神器」といわれ、「終身雇用」「年功賃金」「企業別組合」が含まれる。

Business Tips

CSRとSDGs

CSR(*1)とは「企業の社会的貢献」のことで、企業がステークホルダー（消費者、株主、従業員、地域社会などの利害関係者）から信頼を得るために実施する社会貢献のことです。その取り組みにより企業は成長できるだけでなく、社会の持続性の向上に貢献できます。SDGs(*2)とは「持続可能な開発目標」のことで、国連加盟国全会一致で採択されました。2030年までに持続可能でよりよい世界を目指す国際目標です。いま、企業や地方自治体、NPOなどでもSDGsの視点で活動や組織を見直し、環境・社会問題への取り組みは責任から事業へ移る動きが見られます。

Notes　*1 Corporate Social Responsibilities の略である。
　　　　　*2 Sustainable Development Goals の略である。

Unit 4 — Job Description 仕事の内容

Part 1 In Person

SCENE

Elec International社に就職した良太は、国際営業部に配属され、社会人としての第一歩を踏み出しました。共同プロジェクトの一員として米国のEco Motors社から開発部門に赴任している技術者Mary Smithとランチをしています。

1 ▶ Vocabulary Building　26

[1] 次の英語の語句を聞いて日本語の意味と結び付けなさい。

[2] もう一度英語の語句を聞いてそれぞれ発音しなさい。

be on the right track ●　　　　● 部門

challenging ●　　　　● 〜を克服する

counterpart ●　　　　● うまくいっている

division ●　　　　● （同じ立場の）相手

vary ●　　　　● やりがいのある

overcome ●　　　　● さまざまである

2 ▶ Listening（1）　27

良太とMaryのダイアログを聞いて、各設問に対するもっとも適切な答えを選びなさい。

1　What are Ryota and Mary discussing?

A　Japanese business practices.

B　How they feel about their jobs.

C　American corporate culture.

D　How to succeed in their jobs.

2　What does Mary think of her job?

A　She feels she shoulders a lot of the responsibility.

B　She finds it enjoyable.

C　She considers it to be well-paid.

D　She doesn't get along well with the Japanese engineers.

3 ▶ Listening（2）

30

もう一度ダイアログを聞きながら空欄を埋めなさい。

ダイアログが完成したらリピート練習をしなさい。

Ryota: How do you find your job as a ① _____?

Mary: Well, I really enjoy working on the joint project in Japan.

Ryota: I am glad to hear that. I hope this project between our companies ② _____.

Mary: Well, at present it's ③ _____. Let's hope that continues. How about you? Do you enjoy your job in international sales?

Ryota: Oh yes, but maybe because I'm ④ _____, I also find it a bit challenging.

Mary: Don't worry. I'm sure you'll do fine.

Ryota: Do you have any difficulty working with your ⑤ _____ in the Engineering Division?

Mary: No, not really. Everybody seems ⑥ _____. That said, communication is somewhat difficult.

Ryota: Oh really? Why's that?

Mary: Well, language is a bit of a problem, sometimes. English proficiency ⑦ _____ among the Japanese engineers.

Ryota: I see. I suppose there could be cultural differences, as well.

Mary: You're right. But I guess we'll have to work together to ⑧ _____.

4 ▶ Role Play

完成したダイアログを使ってロールプレイ練習をしなさい。

5 ▸ Reading &Writing

次の製造業の組織を見て、各部門・部署名、役職名に相当する英語を下のA〜Mから選びなさい。

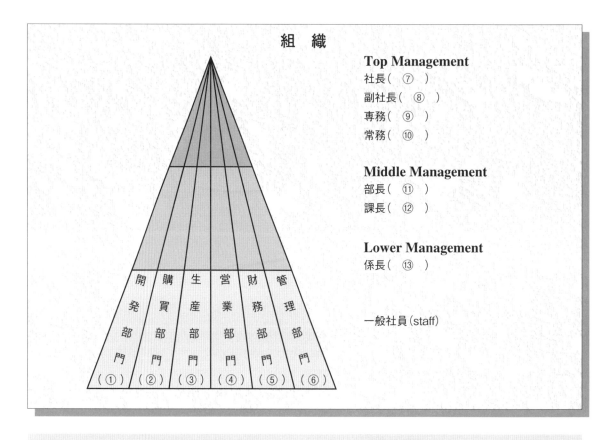

組　織

Top Management
社長（　⑦　）
副社長（　⑧　）
専務（　⑨　）
常務（　⑩　）

Middle Management
部長（　⑪　）
課長（　⑫　）

Lower Management
係長（　⑬　）

一般社員（staff）

開発部門（①）
購買部門（②）
生産部門（③）
営業部門（④）
財務部門（⑤）
管理部門（⑥）

Divisions（部門）

A　Purchasing / Procurement
B　Production / Manufacturing
C　Administration
D　Sales
E　Engineering
F　Finance

Posts（役職）

G　Managing Director
H　Manager
I　President
J　General Manager
K　Assistant Manager
L　Senior Managing Director
M　Vice President

Other Posts

最高経営責任者（Chief Executive Officer / CEO）
最高執行責任者（Chief Operating Officer / COO）
最高財務責任者（Chief Financial Officer / CFO）
会長（Chairman）
監査役（Auditor）

Business Tips

DepartmentとSection

各部門は部（Department）で、各部は課（Section）で構成されています。たとえば、管理部門の中には通常、総務（General Affairs）、人事（Personnel / Human Resources）、法務（Legal）、広報（Public Relations）などの部があります。

Part 2 Telephone Communication

SCENE

良太が応対している電話の相手は、どうやらセールスが目的のようです。ここでは、「**電話の相手の用件を聞き出し、取り次ぎを断るときのコミュニケーション**」のしかたがポイントになります。

1 ▶ Listening (1)

良太と電話の相手のダイアログを聞いて、次の各文の内容が正しければTを、間違っていればFを選びなさい。

1	Ms. Milton is calling on an urgent matter.	T / F
2	Ryota wants to know why Ms. Milton is calling.	T / F
3	Mr. Rock will talk to Ms. Milton later.	T / F

2 ▶ Listening (2)

もう一度ダイアログを聞きながら空欄を埋めなさい。ダイアログが完成したらリピート練習をしなさい。

Ryota: International Sales. Ryota Kimura speaking, can I help you?

Kay: Yes, this is Kay Milton. Could I speak to Mr. Charles Rock, please?

Ryota: Yes, of course.   May I ask what company you are with ?

Kay: Yes. I ①_____ Star Insurance.

Ryota: Thank you, Ms. Milton. And ②_____?(*1)

Kay: Ah, I'd ③_____ if you don't mind.

Ryota: I understand, but he might be better able to assist you if I could give him some idea of

④_____.

Kay: I see, well, I'd like to introduce some of our new products...I'll ⑤_____of his time.

Ryota: OK thank you.   I'll see ⑥_____.(*2)

(*after a minute or so*)

Ryota: I'm sorry, but Mr. Rock ⑦_____ at the moment and can't come to the phone.

Kay: Oh really?

Ryota: If you like, you can leave your telephone number. I'll ⑧_____ if he is interested.

Kay: OK, that's fine.   My number is....

Notes *1 「ご用件は何でしょうか」の表現。
*2 「電話に出られるかどうか聞いてみます」の表現。

3 ▶ Role Play

完成したダイアログを使ってロールプレイ練習をしなさい。

4 ▶ Conversation Map

それぞれの英語のせりふを考えて、電話でのコミュニケーションを成立させなさい。完成したらペアで会話しなさい。

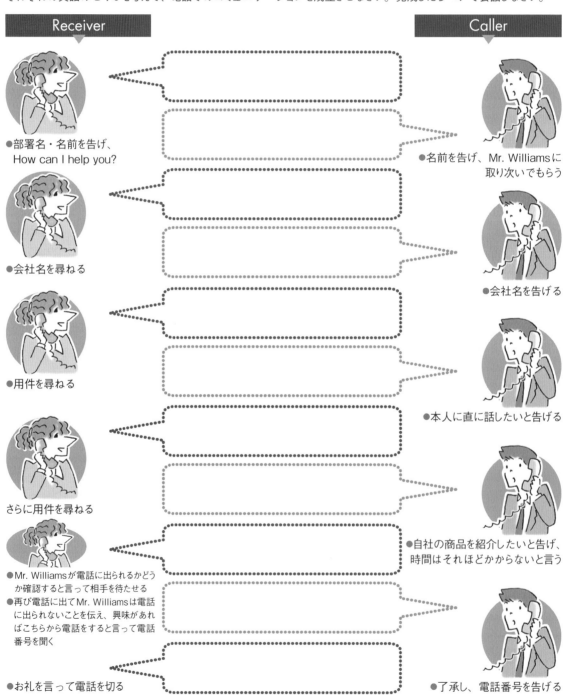

Receiver

● 部署名・名前を告げ、How can I help you?

● 会社名を尋ねる

● 用件を尋ねる

さらに用件を尋ねる

● Mr. Williamsが電話に出られるかどうか確認すると言って相手を待たせる
● 再び電話に出てMr. Williamsは電話に出られないことを伝え、興味があればこちらから電話をすると言って電話番号を聞く

● お礼を言って電話を切る

Caller

● 名前を告げ、Mr. Williamsに取り次いでもらう

● 会社名を告げる

● 本人に直に話したいと告げる

● 自社の商品を紹介したいと告げ、時間はそれほどかからないと言う

● 了承し、電話番号を告げる

Business Topic ▶ ❹

会社の組織

1 次の英文から、「製造会社の組織と部門の役割」を読み取りなさい。

2 音声を聞きながらシャドーイングの練習をしなさい。

The Structure of a Manufacturing Company

A typical manufacturing company is usually made up of divisions each of which have departments, which in turn consist of sections. The following briefly outlines the role of the main divisions in a large manufacturing company. The engineering division designs and develops products. The purchasing division procures parts and components for the products that are then assembled by the production or manufacturing division. The quality division controls and ensures the quality of the products. Finally, the products are sold by the sales division. All divisions are supported by the administration division which includes such departments as planning, market research, legal, general affairs, personnel, public relations and secretarial.

Business Tips

海外生産の進展

日本企業がその生産拠点を海外へ積極的に移転・設立し始めたのは1980年代だと言われています。その後、日本企業の海外生産比率は現在に至るまで着実に増えてきています。海外工場の立ち上げの場合には、現地調査、工事・建設、生産設備の設置などの工場計画の立案から実行、技術移転に係わるさまざまなやり取りや交渉が行われます。また、生産拠点が海外に移るということは、製品を構成する部品やコンポーネントの調達も、ロジスティックスを考えると海外で行う必然性が高まります。このような場面においても英語が必要となるのです。

Unit 5　Email—Announcing a Meeting　会議開催の通知

Part 1　In Person

SCENE

Elec International社とEco Motors社が、共同プロジェクトに
関連した案件を討議するため、日本で会議を開きます。良太は、
その会議のアジェンダ（議事日程）を確定するため、Eco Motors
社のTom Davis取締役にe-mailを送ることになりました。

1 ▶ Vocabulary Building

[**1**] 次の英語の語句を聞いて日本語の意味と結び付けなさい。

[**2**] もう一度英語の語句を聞いてそれぞれ発音しなさい。

agenda ●	● 手伝う・援助する
update ●	● 施設・設備
facility ●	● 議事日程
specifics ●	● 最新の情報を伝える・最新にする
appreciate ●	● 詳細
assist ●	● 宿泊施設
accommodation ●	● 感謝する

2 ▶ Listening（1）

e-mailの内容を音声で聞き、各設問に対するもっとも適切な答えを選びなさい。

1　What is the main purpose of writing the email?

　　A　To thank Eco Motors for their willingness to come to Japan.

　　B　To confirm the topics to be covered at the next meeting.

　　C　To let them know that the hotel has already been booked.

　　D　To confirm what was discussed in the video conference.

2　What was agreed upon at the video conference?

　　A　To expedite the development of the 007 model.

　　B　To exchange emails immediately about the joint project.

　　C　To exchange views on matters regarding the joint project.

　　D　To display the latest 007 model in the Shonan Plant.

3 ▶ Listening（2）

38

もう一度e-mailの内容を聞きながら空欄を埋めなさい。e-mailが完成したらリピート練習をしなさい。

From: Ryota Kimura <ryota@elecxxxx.co.jp>
Date: February 10, 20xx
To: Tom Davis <tdavis@ecoxxxx.com>
Subject: Agenda for the next meeting in Japan

Dear Mr. Davis,

I am writing to ①＿＿＿＿＿＿＿＿＿＿ our upcoming meeting in Japan scheduled from March 1st to March 3rd.

As agreed upon at the video conference yesterday, we would like to discuss issues ②＿＿＿＿＿＿＿＿＿＿ our joint project. We plan to ③＿＿＿＿＿＿＿＿＿＿ the 007 model development. We would also like to take you on ④＿＿＿＿＿＿＿＿＿＿ of our Shonan Plant.

Also, if you could ⑤＿＿＿＿＿＿＿＿＿＿ about what issues you would like to cover in the meeting, we ⑥＿＿＿＿＿＿＿＿＿＿. That would allow us to prepare. Also if you would like us to assist you in reserving accommodations, please let us know ⑦＿＿＿＿＿＿＿＿＿＿.

We look forward to hearing from you soon.

⑧＿＿＿＿＿＿＿＿＿＿,

Ryota Kimura

4 ▶ Repeating

完成したe-mailを使ってリピート練習をしなさい。

5 ▶ Reading &Writing

会議の開催を知らせる社内メールの空欄を下のA～Iの語句を使って埋め、以下の質問に答えなさい。

〈1〉 会議はいつ、どこで開かれ、出席者は誰ですか？

〈2〉 議事は何ですか？

From: Charles Rock <c-rock@elecxxxx.co.jp>
Date: February 14, 20xx
To: the 007 Project Members
Subject: 3 day meeting with Eco Motors in March

Dear Colleagues:

This is to (①) you that we will hold a three-day meeting with Eco Motors at our headquarters from March 1st through 3rd. The (②) of this meeting is to update the (③) of the Power Supply development for the 007 model and to exchange views on (④) issues.

The major items on the agenda include:
1. An update on the progress of the Power Supply development
2. Engineering (⑤) for the 1st prototype of the 007 model
3. A market research report on the demand for EVs
4. Cost (⑥) efforts relative to parts and components
5. Vendor- related matters
6. A plant tour

A more detailed agenda will be (⑦) shortly. All project members are requested to attend this meeting. Please (⑧) that all necessary (⑨) are prepared in advance.

Regards,

Charles Rock
International Sales Department

A	ensure	F	notify
B	circulated	G	status
C	requirements	H	pending
D	materials	I	purpose
E	reduction		

Part **2** Telephone Communication

SCENE

会議中の上司Charles Rock部長にかかってきた電話を田川真理子が受けています。ここでは、電話で「**メッセージを残す・あずかるときのコミュニケーション**」のしかたがポイントになります。

1 ▶ Listening (1)

田川真理子と電話の相手とのダイアログを聞いて、次の各文の内容が正しければTを、間違っていればFを選びなさい。

1 Mr. Rock is away on business.   T / F
2 Mr. Dickinson wants to have a meeting on February 19th.   T / F
3 Mariko will have Mr. Rock call Mr. Dickinson at the hotel.   T / F

2 ▶ Listening (2)

もう一度ダイアログを聞きながら空欄を埋めなさい。ダイアログが完成したらリピート練習をしなさい。

Mariko: Elec International, Mariko Tagawa speaking, how can I help you?

Mr. Dickinson: Hello, ①_____? This is Tony Dickinson of Eco Motors.

Mariko: Just a moment, please...②_____ (*1), Mr. Dickinson. I'm afraid he's in a meeting right now and ③_____ for a while.
④_____? (*2)

Mr. Dickinson: Yes, I'm supposed to meet with him on February 20th, but I'd like to
⑤_____the 19th(*3), if possible. Could you please ask him to
⑥_____ (*4, 5)?

Mariko: Certainly, Mr. Dickinson. Does Mr. Rock have your phone number?

Mr. Dickinson: Ah, I think so, but I'll ⑦_____. It's 060-9102-5573.

Mariko: 060-9102-5573. OK, thank you, Mr. Dickinson. I'll make sure he gets your message(*6).

Mr. Dickinson: Thank you very much. Goodbye.

Mariko: Bye now.

Notes
*1 相手を待たせたときの表現。I'm sorry to have kept you waiting. も使う。
*2 伝言をあずかるときの表現。
*3 予定を繰り上げるときの表現。「約束を繰り下げる」はmove the appointment back。
*4 折り返しの電話を依頼する表現。待つか折り返しの電話を希望するかを確認する場合は、Would you care to wait, or shall I have him call you back?のように聞く。
*5 イギリス英語ではmobile phone が使われる。
*6 メッセージを承ったことを確認する表現。I'll give him your message.などとも言う。

3 ▶ Role Play

完成したダイアログを使ってロールプレイ練習をしなさい。

4 ▶ Conversation Map

それぞれの英語のせりふを考えて、電話でのコミュニケーションを成立させなさい。完成したらペアで会話しなさい。

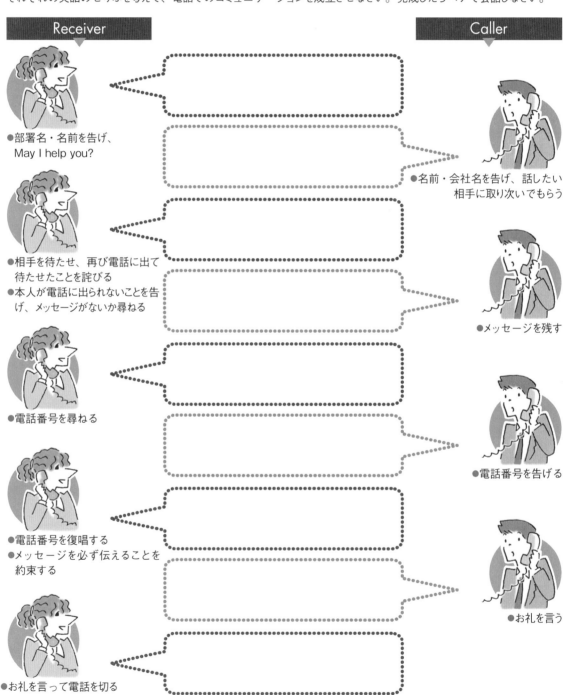

Receiver		Caller

●部署名・名前を告げ、May I help you?

●名前・会社名を告げ、話したい相手に取り次いでもらう

●相手を待たせ、再び電話に出て待たせたことを詫びる
●本人が電話に出られないことを告げ、メッセージがないか尋ねる

●メッセージを残す

●電話番号を尋ねる

●電話番号を告げる

●電話番号を復唱する
●メッセージを必ず伝えることを約束する

●お礼を言う

●お礼を言って電話を切る

Business Topic ▶ ❺

グローバル企業でのコミュニケーション

1 次の英文から、「日本企業と外国企業との共同プロジェクトの目的と近年のコミュニケーションの特徴」を読み取りなさい。

2 音声を聞きながらシャドーイングの練習をしなさい。

Modern International Business Communication

Increasingly, many Japanese companies are conducting joint projects with foreign companies, in a variety of industries. The purpose of this is to produce competitive and marketable products or services in an efficient and inexpensive way by combining the resources of both companies. Members of such international projects therefore often use email to communicate with their counterparts overseas. Within the last decade, email has virtually replaced other means of business communication such as telephones, fax, and snail mail. Furthermore, more and more Japanese companies are holding video conferences with their business partners overseas. Thus, email and video conferencing are essential to modern international business communication.

Business Tips

「内なる国際化」とビジネス通訳

ビジネス通訳とは、産業界、おもに民間企業における通訳であり、経済のグローバル化とともにその需要は高まっています。海外企業と日本企業とのM&A*により、会社組織の「内なる国際化」(経営の意思決定に外国人の役員が参加する状態)が進展した企業では、社内会議での通訳業務ニーズが高まります。具体的には、今までのような外国企業との対外的な通訳だけではなく、株主総会や取締役会などの外国人重役が出席する各種役員会議での同時通訳の需要が発生します。

Notes *「合併と買収」のことであり、Mergers and Acquisitionsの略である。

Unit 6 — Meeting Business Associates at the Airport
ビジネスパートナーを空港で出迎える

Part 1 In Person

SCENE

共同プロジェクトの会議に出席するために来日するEco Motors社開発部門のTom Davis取締役率いる一行を出迎えるために、木村良太は成田空港に来ています。

1 ▶ Vocabulary Building

[1] 次の英語の語句を聞いて日本語の意味と結び付けなさい。

[2] もう一度英語の語句を聞いてそれぞれ発音しなさい。

turbulence ●	● 会社の
jet lag ●	● 長距離
properly ●	● 時差ボケ
adjust ●	● 乱気流
long haul ●	● 十分に
corporate ●	● 順応させる

2 ▶ Listening (1)

空港に到着したTom Davis取締役と出迎えた良太のダイアログを聞いて、各設問に対するもっとも適切な答えを選びなさい。

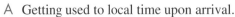

1 What is the time difference between San Francisco and Tokyo?

  A Tokyo is 17 hours behind San Francisco.

  B San Francisco is 9 hours and 10 minutes ahead of Tokyo.

  C San Francisco is 9 hours and 10 minutes behind Tokyo.

  D Tokyo is 17 hours ahead of San Francisco.

2 What adjustment is difficult after a long trip?

  A Getting used to local time upon arrival.

  B Figuring out the local time.

  C Calculating the time difference.

  D Recovering from the fatigue of the trip.

3 ▶ Listening（**2**）

🎧 46

もう一度ダイアログを聞きながら空欄を埋めなさい。
ダイアログが完成したらリピート練習をしなさい。

Ryota: Hello, Mr. Davis. Good to see you again.

Mr. Davis: Hi, Ryota. How are you doing?

Ryota: I am fine, thank you. ① _____?

Mr. Davis: It was all right, ② _____ on the way.

Ryota: Oh really? I hope it wasn't too bad.

Mr. Davis: No, not really. By the way, do you have the time?

Ryota: Yes, it is 9:10 in the evening. You must be very tired. Do you have

　　　③ _____?

Mr.Davis: Well, right now I feel fine, but I'm still on San Francisco time. I hope I'll be able to

　　　④ _____ tonight.

Ryota: I know what you mean. I think San Francisco is ⑤ _____ Tokyo.

Mr.Davis: It is often difficult to ⑥ _____ the new time after

　　　⑦ _____. Oh, here are some of my colleagues.

Ryota: Hello gentlemen, welcome to Japan. We ⑧ _____ outside. We'll take

　　　you to your hotel. This way, please.

Mr.Davis: That is very kind of you. Thanks.

4 ▶ **Role Play**

完成したダイアログを使ってロールプレイ練習をしなさい。

5 ▶ Reading &Writing

[1] Tom Davis 取締役一行の旅程表（Itinerary）です。下のＡ〜Ｈの語句を使って空欄を埋め、質問に答えなさい。

〈 **1** 〉 予定ではサンフランシスコから成田までの飛行時間はどれぐらいか述べなさい（時差は17時間）。

〈 **2** 〉 それぞれの日の予定を述べなさい。

ITINERARY FOR THE TRIP TO JAPAN — The 007 Project Members
February 27 - March 4

<u>MONDAY, FEBRUARY 27 (San Francisco to Tokyo)</u>
18:10　　　　　<u>Leave San Francisco</u>, UAL Flight 837, San Francisco Int'l Airport

<u>TUESDAY, FEBRUARY 28</u>
20:30　　　　　(①), Narita Airport
　　　　　　　Corporate car provided (Mr. Kimura will meet the party at the airport.)
　　　　　　　(②): The Roppongi Tower Hotel
　　　　　　　Phone: 03-5412-11xx

<u>WEDNESDAY, MARCH 1</u>
9 :00-12:00　　Joint Project Meeting at Elec International's Head Office
12:00-13:30　　Lunch
13:30-17:00　　Two separate meetings: (③) and Engineering Mtg.

<u>THURSDAY, MARCH 2</u>
7:30　　　　　Hotel to Shonan Plant by corporate car
9:00-12:00　　Joint Project Meeting at Shonan Plant
12:00-13:30　　Lunch
13:30-17:00　　(④) & Manufacturing meeting
18:00　　　　　(⑤) hosted by Elec Int'l at Japanese restaurant in Shonan

<u>FRIDAY, MARCH 3</u>
9 :00-12:00　　Joint Project Meeting at Head Office
12:00-13:00　　Lunch
13:00-14:30　　(⑥) meeting
15:30　　　　　Office to Narita Airport, (⑦)
19:40　　　　　(⑧), UAL Flight 838, Narita Airport
11:00　　　　　Arrive San Francisco, San Francisco Int'l Airport

A	Corporate car provided.	C	Leave Tokyo	E	Arrive Tokyo	G	Facility tour
B	Accommodation	D	Wrap-up	F	Dinner	H	Sales Mtg.

Part **2**　Telephone Communication

SCENE

Elec International社のCharles Rock部長が電話を受けて工場見学の日程確認をしています。ここでは、「**本人が電話に出て受け答えをするときのコミュニケーション**」のしかたがポイントとなります。

1 ▶ Listening（1）

国際営業部のCharles Rock部長と湘南工場生産部門の井関太郎常務のダイアログを聞いて、次の各文の内容が正しければTを、間違っていればFを選びなさい。

1　Taro Iseki is calling Charles Rock back.　　　　　T / F

2　Charles Rock will not be at Shonan Plant tomorrow.　　　T / F

3　Charles Rock is not happy about Taro's attitude.　　　T / F

2 ▶ Listening（2）

もう一度ダイアログを聞きながら空欄を埋めなさい。ダイアログが完成したらリピート練習をしなさい。

Taro: Could I speak to Mr. Rock, please?

Charles: Speaking.(*1)　What can I do for you?

Taro: Oh, hello, Charles.　This is Taro Iseki of Production.　You called me this morning, but I ① _____ .

Charles: Ah, hello, Taro.　I'm glad ② _____ (*2). Well, I wanted to ③ _____ the facility tour at the Shonan Plant.

Taro: Ah, that's tomorrow, starting at 2:00 p.m., isn't it?

Charles: Yes, that's right.　We'll have a meeting there in the morning, and after lunch, I'd like you to ④ _____ .

Taro: Yes, we'll be ready.　Don't worry.　I've already ⑤ _____ tomorrow's plant tour for Eco Motors' employees.

Charles: Oh, thank you.　It sounds like you've got everything ⑥ _____ .　OK then, see you tomorrow.

Taro: See you tomorrow, Charles.　Bye.

Notes　*1　本人が出て自分であることを伝える表現。This is he. とも言える。
　　　　　　*2　「折り返し電話をかける」の意味。

3 ▶ Role Play

完成したダイアログを使ってロールプレイ練習をしなさい。

4 ▶ Conversation Map

それぞれの英語のせりふを考えて、電話でのコミュニケーションを成立させなさい。完成したらペアで会話しなさい。

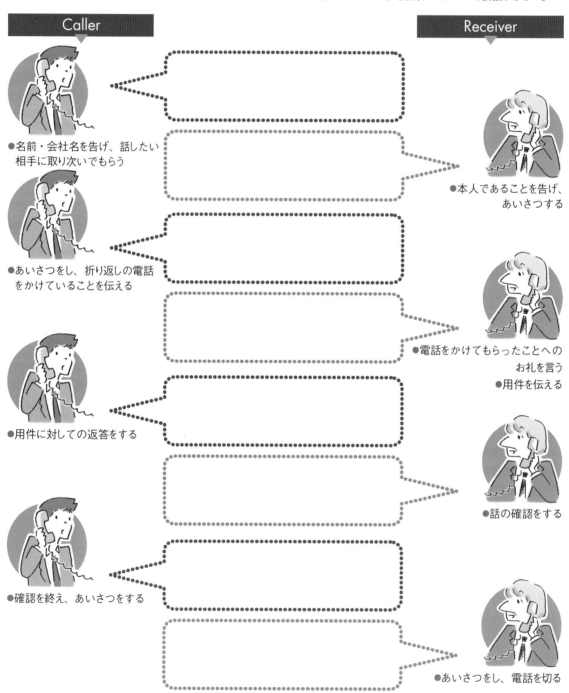

Caller

- 名前・会社名を告げ、話したい相手に取り次いでもらう
- あいさつをし、折り返しの電話をかけていることを伝える
- 用件に対しての返答をする
- 確認を終え、あいさつをする

Receiver

- 本人であることを告げ、あいさつする
- 電話をかけてもらったことへのお礼を言う
- 用件を伝える
- 話の確認をする
- あいさつをし、電話を切る

Business Topic ▶ ❻

出入国手続き

1 次の英文から、「海外出張時の出入国手続きの流れ」を読み取りなさい。

2 音声を聞きながらシャドーイングの練習をしなさい。

Departure and Arrival Procedures

It is advisable that passengers check in at least two hours before their departure when traveling overseas. This is to allow time to request seats and check in all luggage except for carry-on bags. At that time, passengers receive boarding passes and baggage claim tags. After that, they proceed to the security check and passport control. On board passengers fill out a customs declaration form and a landing card. At the destination they go through passport control and visa check. Then, they go to the baggage claim and pick up their luggage. Finally, they line up for a baggage inspection at customs.

Business Tips

旅行者血栓症

飛行機などで長時間同じ姿勢でいるときなどに発症するのが旅行者血栓症*です。この疾患は、血流が悪くなりできた血栓が肺の静脈を詰まらせてしまうことで発症します。列車で長時間座って移動する場合や、オフィスでのデスクワーク、長時間の会議などでも発症することもあります。予防対策として、脱水を防ぐための水分摂取、歩行などの運動や下肢の循環を良好にするためのマッサージが挙げられます。アルコールなどの利尿作用のある飲料ではむしろ脱水が助長され、血液粘度を上昇させることになります。

Notes *英語では、travel thrombosisと呼ぶ。正式名称は「深部静脈血栓症」(deep vein thrombosis)であり、当初は「エコノミークラス症候群」(economy class syndrome)と呼ばれた。

Unit 7　At the Reception Desk　受付での対応

Part 1　In Person

SCENE

共同プロジェクトの会議に出席するために来日したEco Motors
社の一行が、東京にあるElec International社の本社ビルに
到着し、受付でアポイントメントがあることを伝えています。

1 ▶ Vocabulary Building　50

[1] 次の英語の語句を聞いて日本語の意味と結び付けなさい。

[2] もう一度英語の語句を聞いてそれぞれ発音しなさい。

colleague ●　　　　　● 用紙

expect ●　　　　　● 記入する

fill out ●　　　　　● 待つ・期待する

form ●　　　　　● (作業などが)済んだ

done ●　　　　　● 同僚

2 ▶ Listening (1)　51

受付でのダイアログを聞いて、各設問に対するもっとも適切な答えを選びなさい。

1　**What time did Mr. Davis and his colleagues probably arrive at Elec International?**
　A　At 9 o'clock.　52
　B　A few minutes after 9.
　C　They don't make it.
　D　At 8: 40.

2　**How will Mr. Davis and his colleagues find the meeting room?**　53
　A　The receptionist has just explained how to get there.
　B　They will take the elevator by themselves to the meeting room.
　C　A member of the International Sales staff will take them there.
　D　They will take the stairs with Ryota to the meeting room.

3 ▶ Listening(2)

54

もう一度ダイアログを聞きながら空欄を埋めなさい。
ダイアログが完成したらリピート練習をしなさい。

Receptionist: May I help you, sir?

Mr. Davis: Hello, I am Tom Davis of Eco Motors. We ①_____ Mr. Rock in
the International Sales Department at 9 today.

Receptionist: Oh yes, Mr. Davis. We ②_____ you.

Mr. Davis: We are a little early. We'd be happy to wait if he's not ready for us.

Receptionist: No problem. Could you ③_____ this visitor's form, please? I
will have someone take you to the meeting room.

Mr. Davis: ④_____, thank you.

Receptionist: Hello, this is Kyoko Tanaka at reception. Mr. Davis and his colleagues are here.
Can you send someone down here, please?

Mr. Davis: Here you go. We ⑤_____ this form.

Receptionist: Thank you. Please ⑥_____. A member of the International
Sales staff ⑦_____ you in a minute.

Mr. Davis: Thank you.

(*A few minutes later.*)

Ryota: Good morning, Mr. Davis. Welcome to our head office.

Mr. Davis: Hi, Ryota. How are you?

Ryota: Very well, thanks. We ⑧_____ upstairs.
Let me take you there. There is an elevator around the corner.

Mr. Davis: Thank you.

4 ▶ Role Play

完成したダイアログを使ってロールプレイ練習をしなさい。

5 ▶ Reading &Writing

[1] オフィスや工場で見られる掲示文です。下のA〜Jの語句を使って空欄を埋め、日本語の意味に合うように完成させなさい。

〈1〉 ほかにどのような掲示文があるか調べてみよう。

(①) AREA	（立ち入り禁止区域）
(②) NO FIRE	（可燃物・火気厳禁）
(③) PERSONNEL ONLY	（関係者以外立ち入り禁止）
NO SMOKING EXCEPT IN (④) AREAS	（喫煙所以外禁煙）
(⑤) REPAIR	（修理中）
(⑥) ONLY	（従業員専用）
NO (⑦)	（無断立ち入り禁止）
DANGEROUS (⑧) PROHIBITED	（危険物持ち込み禁止）
(⑨) ALL VISITORS MUST REPORT AT THE OFFICE	（通告・すべての訪問者はオフィスで受付すること）
(⑩) REQUIRED BEYOND THIS POINT	（ここから先は身分証明証が必要です）

A	OBJECTS	F	I.D. BADGES
B	EMPLOYEES	G	FLAMMABLES
C	AUTHORIZED	H	NOTICE
D	UNDER	I	TRESPASSING
E	RESTRICTED	J	DESIGNATED

Part 2　Telephone Communication

SCENE

Eco Motors社のTom Davis取締役は、出張先の東京からアメリカにいる部下のボイスメールにメッセージを残しています。ここでは、「ボイスメールにメッセージを残すときのコミュニケーション」のしかたがポイントになります。

1 ▶ Listening (1)

Tom Davis取締役がアシスタントのAnnにメッセージを残すダイアログを聞いて、次の各文の内容が正しければTを、間違っていればFを選びなさい

1	Ann Roberts has the day off today.	T / F
2	Tom asked Ann Roberts to return his call the following day.	T / F
3	Ann Roberts quickly followed Tom's instructions.	T / F

2 ▶ Listening (2)

もう一度ダイアログを聞きながら空欄を埋めなさい。ダイアログが完成したらリピート練習をしなさい。

Recording: "Hello, ①＿＿＿＿＿＿＿＿＿ the voice mail of Ann Roberts. I'm afraid ②＿＿＿＿＿＿＿＿＿ right now. Please leave your name, telephone number and your ③＿＿＿＿＿＿＿＿＿. I'll get back to you as soon as I can. Thank you for calling." (*1)

Tom: Hi Ann, this is Tom ④＿＿＿＿＿＿＿＿＿. Elec International wants to know if we could ⑤＿＿＿＿＿＿＿＿＿ the delivery date for Power-Supply components by two weeks. Can you check with Peter if such a delay would affect our test schedule, and ⑥＿＿＿＿＿＿＿＿＿ A.S.A.P.? It's now 8:50 a.m. Japan time. Please call me at their head office, ⑦＿＿＿＿＿＿＿＿＿.(*2) This is very urgent. Bye.

(*After a while, Ann calls Tom*)

Ann: Hi, Tom. I ⑧＿＿＿＿＿＿＿＿＿ and talked to Peter about it. A ten-working-day extension will be fine ⑨＿＿＿＿＿＿＿＿＿.

Tom: Great, thanks Ann. I'll tell them that.

Notes *1 voice mailは、音声による自分宛てのメッセージを電話で聞いたり、転送したり、一斉送信したりできるサービスで、留守番電話より多くの機能を持つ。

*2 自分への連絡先をメッセージにはっきりと残しておくことが大事。たとえ相手が自分の電話番号を知っていても、メッセージに残すことでより早い相手の対応につながる。I think you have my number, but just in case, it is xxx.のように言うとよい。

3 ▶ Role Play

完成したダイアログを使ってロールプレイ練習をしなさい。

4 ▶ Conversation Map

それぞれの英語のせりふを考えて、電話でのコミュニケーションを成立させなさい。完成したらペアで会話しなさい。

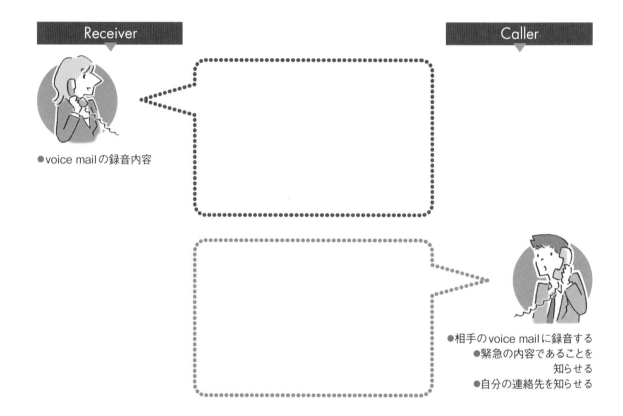

Receiver

● voice mail の録音内容

Caller

● 相手の voice mail に録音する
● 緊急の内容であることを
知らせる
● 自分の連絡先を知らせる

就活・留学準備の強力な味方！

あなたのグローバル英語力を測定

新時代のオンラインテスト

銀行のセミナー・研修にも使われています

CNN ®

GLENTS

留学・就活により役立つ新時代のオンラインテスト

最新
日米口語辞典
[決定版]

エドワード・G・サイデンステッカー＋
松本道弘＝共編

A5判変型（196mm×130mm）函入り 1312ページ

定価5280円（税込）

累計50万部のベストセラー辞典

待望の改訂新版!

- 表現の羅列ではなく、解説を読んで楽しめる辞典
- 硬い辞書訳から脱却し、日常的な口語表現を採用
- ニュアンスや使い分けを詳しく説明
- 「付属する『歩きスマホ』など、今時の言葉を多数増補

鳥飼玖美子 先生
（立教大学名誉教授）

福岡伸一 先生
（生物学者）

推薦!

ENGLISH EXPRESS

音声ダウンロード付き 毎月6日発売 B5判 定価1263円（税込）

これが世界標準の英語!!

CNNの生音音声で学べる唯一の月刊誌

◇ CNNのニュース、インタビューが聴ける
◇ 英語脳に切り替わる同題集付き
◇ カリスマ講師・関正生の文法解説や
　人気通訳者・橋本美穂などの豪華連載も

定期購読をお申し込み
の方には本誌1号分
無料ほか、特典多数!

Business Topic ▶ ❼

国際ビジネスで大切なホスピタリティの精神

1 次の英文から、「国際ビジネスをうまくやるには何が大切か、またどのような準備が求められるか」を読み取りなさい。

2 音声を聞きながらシャドーイングの練習をしなさい。

The Importance of Hospitality in Business Dealings

Good interpersonal relationships are very important in business, as they form the basis for our ability to negotiate effectively. In other words, skill in dealing with human relationships is key to maximizing business performance. Strong interpersonal relationships lay the foundation for the successful launch of joint projects or ventures with business partners. Hospitality is an invaluable factor in every aspect of business dealings, and is thus important for individual customers and to businesses. Therefore, it is vital to understand the major role played by hospitality. Consequently, it is essential not only to learn etiquette but also to cultivate a spirit of hospitality in international business settings.

Part 1 In Person

SCENE

Elec International社とEco Motors社の共同プロジェクト会
議の開催を前に、出席者間で名刺交換が行われています。

1 ▶ Vocabulary Building　58

[**1**]　次の英語の語句を聞いて日本語の意味と結び付けなさい。

[**2**]　もう一度英語の語句を聞いてそれぞれ発音しなさい。

business card ●	● 有能な
fortunate ●	● 光栄に思わせる
competent ●	● 軽い飲食物
flatter ●	● 名刺
refreshments ●	● （水以外の）飲み物
beverage ●	● 幸運な

2 ▶ Listening（1）　59

会議出席者のダイアログを聞いて、各設問に対するもっとも適切な答えを選びなさい。

1　Who is being introduced to the president of Elec International?
- A　Mr. Charles Rock.
- B　Mr. Tom Davis.
- C　Mr. Akira Tani.
- D　Mr. Tony Dickinson.

2　What has Ryota probably prepared?
- A　Soft drinks, spaghetti, and sweets.
- B　Coffee, tea, and dim sum.
- C　Drinks and light snacks.
- D　Cocktails, beer, and fruit.

3 ▶ Listening (2)

62

もう一度ダイアログを聞きながら空欄を埋めなさい。
ダイアログが完成したらリピート練習をしなさい。

Charles: Good to see you again, Tom.

Tom: Hi, Charles. How are you?

Charles: Pretty good, thanks. Hey, ① _____ Mr. Tani, president of Elec International.

Tom: Oh, great. I haven't had a chance to meet him yet.

Charles: Mr. Tani, this is Mr. Tom Davis from Eco Motors. He is the Eco Motors' leader of the 007 project.

Tom: It's ② _____, Mr. Tani. Let me give you my business card.

Mr. Tani: Nice to meet you too, Mr. Davis. And here's mine.

Tom: Thank you very much.

Mr.Tani: I've heard good things about you from Charles. I ③ _____ a competent leader like you on this project.

Tom: Thank you. ④ _____. I feel ⑤ _____ your excellent team.

Charles: Well, gentlemen, Ryota ⑥ _____ for us. Please ⑦ _____ some beverages, water, fruit and snacks.

Tom: ⑧ _____ him. I appreciate it.

4 ▶ Role Play

完成したダイアログを使ってロールプレイ練習をしなさい。

5 ▶ Reading &Writing

[1] 次の名刺について、下のA～Dの語句を使って空欄を埋め、質問に答えなさい。

〈 1 〉 3人についてわかることを述べなさい。

〈 2 〉 Elec International 社の社員になったつもりで、自分の名刺を書いてみよう（所属・肩書きは自由に）。

 Eco Motors

Tony Dickinson
Manager
International Purchasing Department

220 West Milford Dr.   (408)529-27xx, (408)529-28xx (Fax)
San Jose, (①)   jbrown@ecoxxxx.com

Taro Iseki
Managing Director
Manufacturing Division

ELEC INTERNATIONAL CORPORATION
(②)

10 Sugahara, Fujisawa-shi, Kanagawa-ken, 252 -0068 Japan
Tel: 0466-48-55xx, Fax: 0466-48-56xx
E-mail: t-iseki@elecxxxx.com

 Eco Motors

Tom Davis, (③)
(④)
Engineering Division

220 West Milford Dr.   (408)529-27xx, (408)529-28xx (Fax)
San Jose, CA 95134   tdavis@ecoxxxx.com

A	Ph.D	C	Director
B	Shonan Plant	D	CA 95134

Part **2** Telephone Communication

SCENE

Eco Motors社のTony Dickinson氏はElec International社の
Charles Rock部長に電話をかけ、会議前のミーティングのアポイントを取ろうとしています。ここでは、「**電話でアポイントメントを取りつけるときのコミュニケーション**」のしかたがポイントになります。

1 ▶ Listening（1）

Tony Dickinson氏とCharles Rock部長の会話です。ダイアログを聞いて、次の各文の内容が正しければTを、間違っていればFを選びなさい。

1 Tony will meet Charles after the staff meeting tomorrow.　　T / F

2 They will discuss business over lunch tomorrow.　　T / F

3 They will have breakfast at Napoli tomorrow morning.　　T / F

2 ▶ Listening（2）

もう一度ダイアログを聞きながら空欄を埋めなさい。ダイアログが完成したらリピート練習をしなさい。

Charles: International Sales, Charles Rock speaking.

Tony: Hi, Charles. This is Tony Dickinson of Eco Motors. How are you doing?

Charles: Tony! Good to ①_____! How is the staff meeting going ?

Tony: Great. Look, I ②_____ you had any time to spare. I'd like to discuss some matters with you.

Charles: Sure, that's fine. ③_____ ?(*1)

Tony: ④_____ a breakfast meeting(*2) tomorrow morning?

Charles: Well, ⑤_____ a working lunch (*3), instead, if you don't mind.

Tony: OK, that ⑥_____ me. When and where shall we meet?

Charles: Let's see.... How about *Napoli*, the Italian restaurant on the 2nd floor at 12:30?

Tony: ⑦_____. Look forward to seeing you then.

Charles: OK then, see you tomorrow.

Notes *1 相手にいつがよいか都合を聞く表現。ほかに、When will suit you?など。
*2 会議（商談）を兼ねた朝食。
*3 会議（商談）を兼ねた昼食。business lunch、power lunchとも言う。

3 ▸ Role Play

完成したダイアログを使ってロールプレイ練習をしなさい。

4 ▸ Conversation Map

それぞれの英語のせりふを考えて、電話でのコミュニケーションを成立させなさい。完成したらペアで会話しなさい。

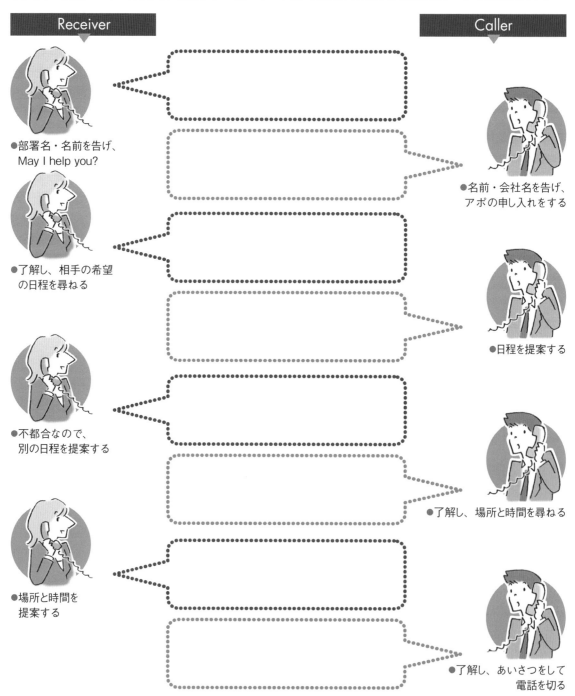

Receiver

● 部署名・名前を告げ、
May I help you?

● 了解し、相手の希望
の日程を尋ねる

● 不都合なので、
別の日程を提案する

● 場所と時間を
提案する

Caller

● 名前・会社名を告げ、
アポの申し入れをする

● 日程を提案する

● 了解し、場所と時間を尋ねる

● 了解し、あいさつをして
電話を切る

Business Topic ▶ ⑧

異文化間コミュニケーション

1 次の英文から、「国際ビジネスにおいて異文化コミュニケーション対応が重要である理由」を読み取りなさい。

2 音声を聞きながらシャドーイングの練習をしなさい。

65

Intercultural Communication in Business Environments

Simply put, intercultural communication is defined as communication between persons from different cultural backgrounds. There is no doubt that communication methods are substantially influenced by culture. Currently, globalization is bringing together companies of different nations on a larger scale than ever to conduct business. As a result, many workplaces are rapidly becoming multicultural. The need for effective intercultural communication is now becoming more important in all aspects of business communication. Therefore, success in such business environments is largely attributable to learning the art of cultural mediation. For this reason, it is important to consider not only language barriers, but also cultural differences that affect both business and interpersonal communication.

Business Tips

国際ビジネスと世界諸英語

英語は現在、国際共通言語として、大切な役割を担っています。ただし、英語の国際的普及は英語の多様化をもたらしており、専門家はこのような現代英語の姿を世界諸英語（World Englishes）とかグローバル諸英語（Global Englishes）と呼んでいます。世界の多くの人びとは自国の言語文化のなかで英語を学び、各国特有のさまざまな英語を使用しています。私たちはビジネスを通して世界の人びとと交流するなかで、いろいろな英語に出会います。この様な現代英語の現状と特徴を理解して国際ビジネスに臨むことが大切です。

Unit 9 Opening Remarks at a Meeting
会議冒頭のあいさつ

Part 1 In Person

SCENE

3日間の共同プロジェクト会議がはじまり、Elec International 社の谷社長、岡部長、Eco Motors 社の Tom Davis 取締役ほか、主要メンバーが出席しています。司会は田川真理子課長が担当しています。

1 ▶ Vocabulary Building

[1] 次の英語の語句を聞いて日本語の意味と結び付けなさい。

[2] もう一度英語の語句を聞いてそれぞれ発音しなさい。

adjustment ●   ● （〜の要求を）受け入れる

accommodate ●   ● 最新情報

follow ●   ● 依頼する

break ●   ● 続く

update ●   ● 中断する

call on ●   ● 調整

2 ▶ Listening（1）

会議の冒頭のダイアログを聞いて、各設問に対するもっとも適切な答えを選びなさい。

1 **What is Mariko's role at the meeting?**

  A Recording secretary.

  B Presenter.

  C Timekeeper.

  D Moderator.

2 **What is the first item on the agenda for today?**

  A The 007 key components development.

  B Mr. Tani's opening remarks.

  C Mr. Davis's closing address.

  D The market research results.

3 ▶ Listening（2）

70

もう一度ダイアログを聞きながら空欄を埋めなさい。
ダイアログが完成したらリピート練習をしなさい。

Mariko: First, let me explain the schedule for our three day meeting. If you'd like to
① _____ , please let us know and we will do our best to
② _____ .

Mr. Davis: That sounds great. Thanks.

Mariko: As you can see on the agenda on the screen, we'll ③ _____ from our
president, Mr. Tani, and we would also like to invite Mr. Davis to say a few words.

Mr. Davis: I'd be happy to.

Mariko: Thank you, Mr. Davis. ④ _____ is our team's presentation on the
progress of the key components development. This will ⑤ _____
a presentation on the market research results from Eco Motors. We will then
⑥ _____ for an hour and a half. ....

Mr. Davis: Thank you for ⑦ _____ the agenda, Mariko. The schedule seems to
cover everything perfectly.

Mariko: Good. Then, I'd like to ⑧ _____ Mr. Tani for his address.

Mr. Tani: Of course. Thank you, Mariko. Good morning everyone and welcome....

4 ▶ Role Play

完成したダイアログを使ってロールプレイ練習をしなさい。

5 ▶ Reading &Writing

[1] 会議の冒頭のあいさつについて、下のA〜Hの語句を使って空欄を埋め、質問に答えなさい。

〈**1**〉 谷社長は、両社の共同プロジェクトを成功させるには何が必要と述べているか?

〈**2**〉 谷社長の今日の予定を述べなさい。

Opening Remarks by President Tani
(谷社長による会議冒頭のあいさつの続き)

Many thanks for coming all the way from America to (①) this joint project meeting
(②). I hope you are not too tired from the long flight. I'd also like to take this
opportunity to (③) the excellent job you have done to date.

My belief is that open communication is (④) in an international project like ours.
Open communication allows us to exchange information and share any questions or
concerns promptly before they become problems.

(⑤) I believe that this is the opportune time to have this three day meeting. I think it's
also important to keep in mind that the top management of both our companies
(⑥) this project.

I need to let you know, however, that I'll have to (⑦) after the morning session today
because of (⑧). But I plan to meet you again at dinner tomorrow evening. I am
looking forward to talking to you individually then.

Thank you.

A	a prior commitment	E	take part in
B	from this perspective	F	the key to success
C	complement you all on	G	despite your busy schedules
D	excuse myself	H	have high expectations for

Part **2** Telephone Communication

SCENE

Eco Motors社から湘南工場・開発部門に駐在しているエンジニアのMaryが、上司のTomに電話で会議に遅れそうなことを伝えています。ここでは、「**会議に遅れることを伝えるときのコミュニケーション**」のしかたがポイントとなります。

1 ▶ Listening (1)

MaryとTomのダイアログを聞いて、次の各文の内容が正しければTを、間違っていればFを選びなさい。

1 Mary does not plan to attend the meeting today   T / F

2 Mary is expecting to get the data necessary for the meeting.   T / F

3 Tom is upset about the call from Mary.   T / F

2 ▶ Listening (2)

もう一度ダイアログを聞きながら空欄を埋めなさい。ダイアログが完成したらリピート練習をしなさい。

Tom : Tom Davis speaking.

Mary : Hi, Tom. This is Mary. Could I talk to you for a second?

Tom : Sure, Mary. ① _____ ?

Mary : Well, this is ② _____ the afternoon session today.(*1)

     I'm afraid I ③ _____ .(*2)

Tom : Really? Is everything OK?

Mary : Yes, everything's fine, but I haven't got the whole set of ④ _____ ready

     yet. I don't think it'll take too long to ⑤ _____ .

     Maybe I'll be late by half an hour ⑥ _____ .

Tom : OK, don't worry. There's a lot to discuss at the meeting and we can

     ⑦ _____ . Why don't you ⑧ _____ and take care of the

     data first?

Mary : OK, I'll do that. Thanks for ⑨ _____ .

Tom: That's no problem, Mary. See you in the meeting.

Mary : See you later.

Notes   *1 「〜に関してのことです」の表現。I'm calling about〜とも言える。

       *2 「申しわけありませんが、〜かもしれません」の表現。

3 ▶ Role Play

完成したダイアログを使ってロールプレイ練習をしなさい。

4 ▶ Conversation Map

それぞれの英語のせりふを考えて、電話でのコミュニケーションを成立させなさい。完成したらペアで会話しなさい。

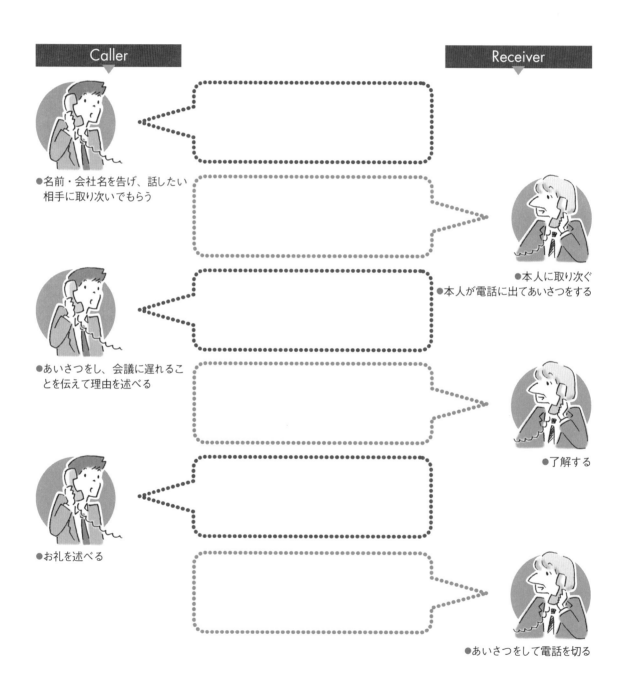

Business Topic ▸ ❾

訪日外国人を増やすための政府の取り組み

1 次の英文から、「訪日外国人数の推移、訪日外国人を増やす政府の施策」を読み取りなさい。

2 音声を聞きながらシャドーイングの練習をしなさい。

Government Efforts to Increase the Number of Foreign Visitors to Japan

Overall, more and more foreigners are visiting Japan in accordance with the government policy of making Japan a tourism-oriented nation. According to JTA[*1], the number of people visiting Japan surged from 679,900 in 2009 to 31,190,000 in 2019. Recently, however, there has been a marked decline in the number of people traveling abroad due to the pandemic[*2] in 2020. Nevertheless, from a medium-term perspective, the exchange of personnel across borders is expected to show a recovery. In an attempt to attract businesses, the government is simultaneously engaged in the promotion of MICE, wherein M represents meetings held by corporations; I stands for incentive which includes incentive or training travels on business; C stands for conferences held by international organizations or academic societies; and E stands for exhibitions including trade fairs.

*1 JTA はJapan Tourism Agency の略で観光庁を指す。同庁は国土交通省の外局で、「観光立国」の推進体制を強化するために 2008 年に設立された。
*2 世界的に流行の病気

Business Tips

M&Aと提携

最近は、M&A (Mergers and Acquisitions) という言葉をよく耳にするようになりました。これは「合併と買収」のことです。合併の場合は合併される会社は消滅しますが、買収の場合は買収される会社の株主は変わりますが、その会社は存続します。また提携とは他社と協力関係を築くことで、業務提携と資本提携があります。M&Aに比べ、企業の自立性が維持されるという特徴があります。日本企業と外国企業とのM&Aも提携も着実に増加しています。

Unit 10 Presentation プレゼンテーション

Part 1 In Person

SCENE

Elec International社のプレゼンがはじまりました。開発部の岡弘部長がEco Motors社に依頼されて開発しているPower-Supply component（高性能電池システム）の開発の進捗について説明しています。

1 ▸ Vocabulary Building

74

[1] 次の英語の語句を聞いて日本語の意味と結び付けなさい。

[2] もう一度英語の語句を聞いてそれぞれ発音しなさい。

chart ● ● 基準
prototype ● ● 特性・特徴
table ● ● 図表
durability ● ● 表・一覧表
criterion ● ● 試作
chronological ● ● 耐久性
feature ● ● 時系列の

2 ▸ Listening (1)

75

岡部長のプレゼンテーションを聞いて、各設問に対するもっとも適切な答えを選びなさい。

1 **What test has Elec International finished most recently?**

76

   A The durability test on the 1st prototype model.

   B The power requirements test on the EV model.

   C The performance test on the 2nd prototype.

   D The performance test on some EV parts.

2 **What is not included in Mr. Oka's presentation at this point?**

77

   A Features of competitors' models.

   B Improvements made on the second prototype.

   C The first development schedule.

   D Cost related issues.

3 ▸ Listening (2)

78

もう一度ダイアログを聞きながら空欄を埋めなさい。
ダイアログが完成したらリピート練習をしなさい。

Mr. Oka: ①_____ my presentation is to update you on the development of the
Power-Supply component for the 007 electric vehicle model.

②_____ the original development schedule. As highlighted here,
we have just conducted a performance test on the second prototype model of Power-
Supply.

③_____ that the model meets the power requirements. As for
durability, we have fallen slightly short of our target. But I am certain that we can
rectify this and reach the target in time.

④_____ improvements made on each engineering criterion in
chronological order.

⑤_____ the test results of the first and second prototypes.
For your reference, the features of our model are compared with those of our
competitors ⑥_____.

As for the timing of delivery....

4 ▸ Role Play

岡部長になってプレゼンテーションの練習をしなさい。

5 ▶ Reading &Writing

［ 1 ］ 岡部長のプレゼンにそって、以下のスライドに順番をつけなさい。

［ 2 ］ プレゼンではどの種類のグラフ・表を見せながら説明しているのかを英語で記入し、その日本語名も書きなさい。

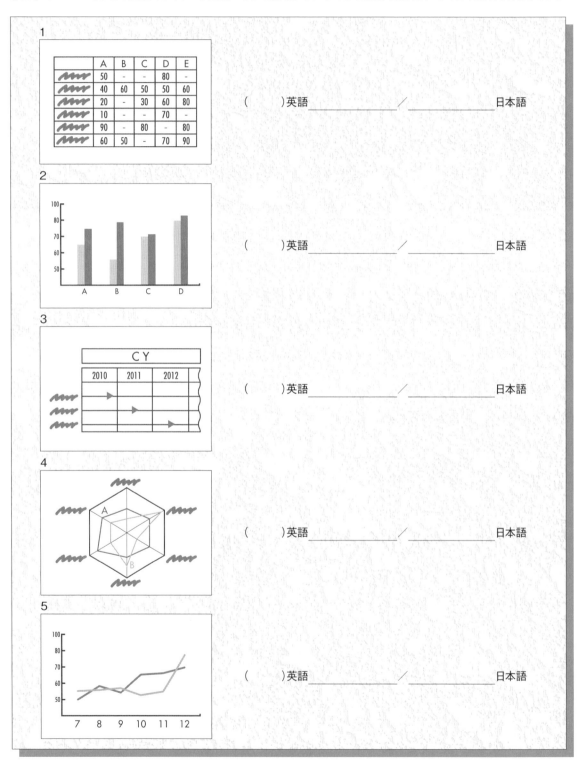

1

（　　　）英語＿＿＿＿＿＿＿＿／＿＿＿＿＿＿＿日本語

2

（　　　）英語＿＿＿＿＿＿＿＿／＿＿＿＿＿＿＿日本語

3

（　　　）英語＿＿＿＿＿＿＿＿／＿＿＿＿＿＿＿日本語

4

（　　　）英語＿＿＿＿＿＿＿＿／＿＿＿＿＿＿＿日本語

5

（　　　）英語＿＿＿＿＿＿＿＿／＿＿＿＿＿＿＿日本語

Part 2 Telephone Communication

SCENE

初日の会議が終わり、Charles Rock部長が岡弘部長に、次の会議前の打ち合わせをお願いしています。ここでは、**「打ち合わせを申し入れるときのコミュニケーション」**のしかたがポイントとなります。

1 ▶ Listening（1）

開発部の岡部長と国際営業部のRock部長が電話で話しています。ダイアログを聞いて、次の各文の内容が正しければTを、間違っていればFを選びなさい。

1 They agree to see each other tomorrow morning.　　T / F
2 They will have a talk at 8:15 tomorrow morning.　　T / F
3 They have several matters to talk about.　　T / F

2 ▶ Listening（2）

もう一度ダイアログを聞きながら空欄を埋めなさい。ダイアログが完成したらリピート練習をしなさい。

Mr. Oka: Hiroshi Oka speaking.

Mr. Rock: Hello, Hiroshi. This is Charles of International Sales.

Mr. Oka: Ah, Charles. ①_____?

Mr. Rock: Well, you ②_____ at today's meeting.

Mr. Oka: Thanks.

Mr. Rock: Anyway, I am calling to see ③_____ before the morning session tomorrow.(*1) We should compare notes on some ④_____.

Mr. Oka: I guess ⑤_____. We ought to reduce the delay of Power-Supply components, and ⑥_____ the supplier immediately.

Mr. Rock: Exactly. ⑦_____ at a quarter to eight?(*2)

Mr. Oka: That's fine. Please come to see me in my office. We can discuss some ⑧_____ then.

Mr. Rock: Yes, that ⑨_____. See you in the morning, then.

Mr. Oka: OK, bye.

Notes *1 I am calling to see if ～（～かどうかと思い電話をかけています）の表現。
*2 「～しませんか」と提案するときの表現。

3 ▸ Role Play

完成したダイアログを使ってロールプレイ練習をしなさい。

4 ▸ Conversation Map

それぞれの英語のせりふを考えて、電話でのコミュニケーションを成立させなさい。完成したらペアで会話しなさい。

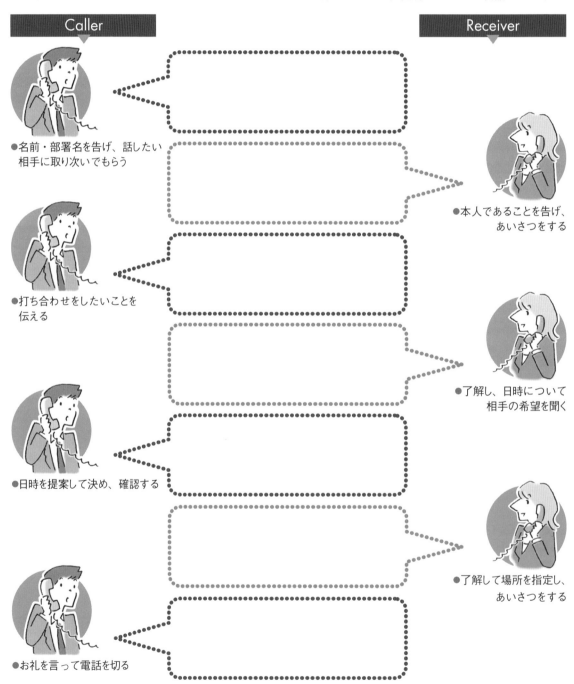

Business Topic ▶ ❿

プレゼンテーションのスキル

1 次の英文から、「プレゼンテーションの準備と実施にあたっての注意点」を読み取りなさい。

2 音声を聞きながらシャドーイングの練習をしなさい。

Giving Presentations

Giving a presentation has two main stages; preparation and performance. Preparation involves having a clear understanding of the goal of the presentation and the intended audience. This will determine the content and outline of the presentation. The next step is to conduct research, and organize findings into categories. After this is complete, findings should be written up and sources should be cited. Performance includes delivering the speech, with a clear introduction, body, and conclusion, and answering questions afterwards. Speed, intonation, and volume are also important for an effective presentation. In addition, eye contact, gestures, and posture play a vital role in making a good impression on the audience.

Business Tips

日本人とプレゼンテーション

プレゼンテーション行う際に、日本人のなかには準備した原稿を取り出して読み上げる人がいます。しかし、本来は出席者の顔を見渡しながら堂々と話すようにするべきでしょう。そのためには、ぶっつけ本番ではなくリハーサルをしておくことが大切です。また、外国企業との会議の冒頭のあいさつでも、準備した原稿を淡々とした口調で読み上げる日本人役員がいます。このような態度は海外のビジネスパーソンによい印象を与えないので避けたいものです。

Unit 11 Negotiation 交渉

Part 1 In Person

SCENE

3日間の共同プロジェクト会議も最終日となりました。
Power-SupplyコンポーネントのEco Motors社へ
の納期について、両社が話し合っています。

1 ▶ Vocabulary Building

[1] 次の英語の語句を聞いて日本語の意味と結び付けなさい。

[2] もう一度英語の語句を聞いてそれぞれ発音しなさい。

impact ●	● 組み立て
vendor ●	● 仕事日・平日
minimize ●	● 時間外に・超過して
get by ●	● 影響・衝撃
overtime ●	● 何とかする
assembly ●	● 〜を最小限にする
exceed ●	● 超える
working day ●	● 納入業者

2 ▶ Listening (1)

両社の担当者がスケジュールの遅れや納期について話し合うダイアログを聞いて、各設問に対するもっとも適切な答え
を選びなさい。

1 **What is the reason for the late delivery of the components to Eco Motors?**

    A Elec International is behind in their production schedule due to a shortage of workers.

    B A supplier is manufacturing some parts later than expected.

    C Elec International has problems with the quality of their components.

    D Eco Motors plans to have the components delivered earlier than originally scheduled.

2 **When will the components most likely be delivered to Eco Motors?**

    A 9 days later than originally planned.

    B According to the original schedule.

    C 10 weeks later than originally scheduled.

    D They will not be delivered for the foreseeable future.

3 ▶ **Listening (2)**

86

もう一度ダイアログを聞きながら空欄を埋めなさい。
ダイアログが完成したらリピート練習をしなさい。

Mr. Davis: I've ① _____ the late delivery of the components with the manager.

Mr. Oka: Oh, really? What did he say?

Mr. Davis: He said that the preparation for the vehicle test ② _____ according
to the original schedule.

Mr. Oka: Well, the problem is that one of our vendors ③ _____.

Mr. Davis: I see. Is there anything you can do about that?

Mr. Oka: Certainly, we'll do whatever's necessary to ④ _____.

Mr. Davis: We could probably ⑤ _____ 10 working days, if we have no
choice.

Mr. Oka: OK, I'll strongly urge the vendor to work extra overtime to
⑥ _____.

Mr. Davis: That's fair enough!

Mr. Oka: We'll ⑦ _____ and ensure that the delay does not exceed 10 working
days.

Mr. Davis: OK, ⑧ _____.

Mr. Oka: Thank you for your understanding on this.

4 ▶ **Role Play**

完成したダイアログを使ってロールプレイ練習をしなさい。

5 ▶ Reading &Writing

次の議事録について、下のA～Hの語句を使って空欄を埋め、それぞれの日本語を考えなさい。

(①) of the Sales Meeting

Companies: Elec International and Eco Motors

(②): The status of cost reduction efforts relative to key parts

Date: March 1st, 20xx

Time: 13:30-17:00

(③): Meeting Room 10 at Head Office

(④): Eco Motors: Tony Dickinson, Manager from Purchasing, ..., ..., ...

　　　　　Elec International: Charles Rock, General Manager from Int'l Sales, ..., ...

	(⑤)	(⑥)	Date
Cost	5% cost reduction target for key parts	Mr. Rock	August 1, 20xx
Vendor	Recommend competitive vendors.	Mr. Dickinson	March 20, 20xx
Volume	Confirm the purchasing volume of Power-Supply components.	Mr. Dickinson	April 1, 20xx
Quality	....	....	....
Delivery	....	....	....

Minutes (⑦) by: Charles Rock　　　　　*Charles Rock*

Minutes (⑧) by: Tony Dickinson　　　　*Tony Dickinson*

A	approved	E	purpose
B	minutes	F	submitted
C	venue	G	decisions and actions
D	responsibility	H	attendees

Part **2** Telephone Communication

SCENE

最後のミーティングに出席できない駐在エンジニアのMaryが
上司のTomに電話をかけています。ここでは、「**ねぎらいと別
れのあいさつのコミュニケーション**」のしかたがポイントとなり
ます。

1 ▶ Listening (1)

別れのあいさつをかわすMaryとTomのダイアログを聞いて、次の各文の内容が正しければTを、間違っていればFを
選びなさい。

1　Mary wants some advice from Tom about her job.　　T / F

2　Tom extends his gratitude to Mary.　　T / F

3　Tom is flying back to the U.S. alone.　　T / F

2 ▶ Listening (2)

もう一度ダイアログを聞きながら空欄を埋めなさい。ダイアログが完成したらリピート練習をしなさい。

Mary: Hello, Tom. This is Mary.

Tom: Oh, Mary. How are you this morning?

Mary: Good, thank you. I was calling to ask if everything is going OK.

Tom: Oh, thank you, Mary. Yes, ①_____. You've been really helpful and

　　　②_____ (*1).

Mary: Thank you for saying so. I am sorry that I won't be able to attend the ③_____

　　　due to an appointment with the suppliers.

Tom: Don't worry, Mary. We'll ④_____.

Mary: Thanks. I'll ⑤_____ our discussions with the suppliers.

Tom: Great. And please call me ⑥_____ or if you need anything.

Mary: I will, thank you. By the way, have a safe trip back home! ⑦_____ the

　　　others.(*2)

Tom: Yes, I will. Thank you for the call. Bye for now.

Notes　*1　感謝の気持ちを表す表現。ほかに、I would like to express/extend appreciation for ～や、I am grateful for ～なども使える。
　　　　*2　「～によろしく」という意味。 Give my (best) regards to～ / Say hello to ～などの表現もある。

3 ▶ Role Play

完成したダイアログを使ってロールプレイ練習をしなさい。

4 ▶ Conversation Map

それぞれの英語のせりふを考えて、電話でのコミュニケーションを成立させなさい。完成したらペアで会話しなさい。

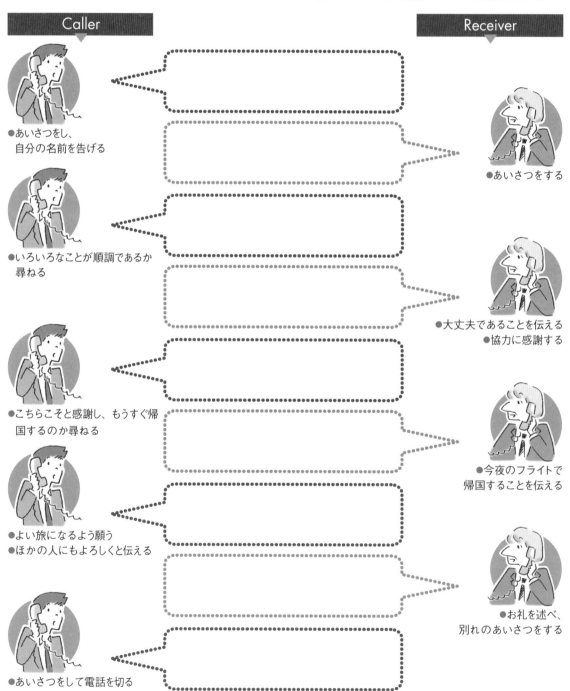

Caller

- あいさつをし、自分の名前を告げる
- いろいろなことが順調であるか尋ねる
- こちらこそと感謝し、もうすぐ帰国するのか尋ねる
- よい旅になるよう願う
- ほかの人にもよろしくと伝える
- あいさつをして電話を切る

Receiver

- あいさつをする
- 大丈夫であることを伝える
- 協力に感謝する
- 今夜のフライトで帰国することを伝える
- お礼を述べ、別れのあいさつをする

Business Topic ▶ ⑪

望ましいネゴシエーションとは？

1 次の英文から、「ビジネスにおいて望ましいネゴシエーションとはどのようなものか」を読み取りなさい。

2 音声を聞きながらシャドーイングの練習をしなさい。

The Art of Negotiation

If a negotiation is seen as a zero-sum game (*1), a participant's gain or loss is balanced by the loss or gain of the other party. It is best, however, if both parties come out of the negotiation in a win-win situation (*2). To achieve this, it is vital to prepare a negotiation strategy and evaluate it comprehensively. Prior to the meeting, it is imperative to reach a consensus in house on what points are open to negotiation and how to prioritize (*3) them. In any negotiation, the outcome is directly affected by the knowledge, abilities and interpersonal skills of the participants. Also, knowledge of the other party is essential to ensure an effective strategy and tactics in the negotiation.

Notes
*1 合計するとゼロになること。すなわち一方の利益が他方の損失になる交渉のこと。
*2 交渉において、何かほかのものをからめることにより、双方が満足感を持てる状態のこと。
*3 ～に優先順位をつける。

Business Tips

コミュニケーションにおける 高文脈依存と低文脈依存

「ハイコンテクスト文化とローコンテクスト文化」は人類学者のE.T.ホールが唱えた概念です。ここでの「コンテクスト」とはコミュニケーションの基盤である言語・共通の知識・体験・価値観などのことです。日本などのハイコンテクスト文化ではコンテクストの共有性が高く、お互いに相手の意図を察しあうことで通じることが頻繁にあります。一方、欧米などのローコンテクスト文化では、コンテクストに依存するのではなく、あくまで言語によりコミュニケーションを図ろうとします。つまり、両者の違いは「コンテクスト依存型」か「言語依存型」ということになります。

Unit 12 Invitation to Dinner 接待

Part 1 In Person

SCENE

共同プロジェクト会議2日目の夜、Elec International社はEco Motors社の一行を料亭「月光」へと食事に招待しています。

1 ▶ Vocabulary Building

90

[1] 次の英語の語句を聞いて日本語の意味と結び付けなさい。

[2] もう一度英語の語句を聞いてそれぞれ発音しなさい。

propose a toast ●　　　　● 繁栄

fruitful ●　　　　● 乾杯の音頭を取る

open up ●　　　　● （機会・可能性など）を切り開く

take the lead in～ ●　　　　● ～の先に立って進める

prosperity ●　　　　● 実りの多い

uplifting ●　　　　● 励みとなる・楽しくさせる

cuisine ●　　　　● 料理

2 ▶ Listening（1）

91

一行を料亭に招待し食事をはじめようとするダイアログを聞いて、各設問に対するもっとも適切な答えを選びなさい。

1 **According to Mr. Oka, what is the role of the 007 project team ?**

92

　A Hosting the welcome banquet.

　B Solving problems associated with the business partnership.

　C Leading joint efforts to create new business opportunities.

　D Minimizing the risk of the 007 project.

2 **What is the general consensus regarding this project?**

93

　A The success of the project is in doubt.

　B The project is likely to be successful.

　C Both companies have low expectations for this project.

　D The project has not been implemented in a timely fashion.

3 ▶ **Listening (2)**

94

もう一度ダイアログを聞きながら空欄を埋めなさい。
ダイアログが完成したらリピート練習をしなさい。

Ryota: First, I'd like to ① _____ ?

Mr. Oka: Of course. Gentlemen, many thanks for your hard work at our meeting. I think it was very ② _____ . I should also mention that our successful cooperation has the potential to ③ _____ in our business.

Tom: Absolutely!

Mr: Oka: It is you, the joint team of the 007 project, who ④ _____ . So I'd like to propose a toast ⑤ _____ this project, ⑥ _____ both our companies, and good health to you all. Cheers!

Others: Cheers!

Tom: Thank you very much for ⑦ _____ .

Ryota: Thank you Mr. Oka. Gentlemen, this restaurant ⑧ _____ . May I briefly explain what we are having tonight?

Tom: Sure, ⑨ _____ , Ryota.

Ryota: The dishes we are having tonight are....

4 ▶ **Role Play**

完成したダイアログを使ってロールプレイ練習をしなさい。

5 ▶ Reading &Writing

[1] 会席料理のお品書きについて、下のA〜Gの説明が該当する料理を選んで空欄を埋め、質問に答えなさい。

〈 1 〉 他にも接待でふるまう日本料理を調べて、英語で説明してみなさい。

会席料理（　Kaiseki: a traditional Japanese multiple course meal　）

先付（sakizuke—前菜）（　①　）

向付（mukozuke—刺身・酢の物など）（　②　）

八寸＊（hassun—四角形の膳［一辺が八寸］に盛られた酒肴）（　③　）

椀盛（wanmori—肉や魚と野菜などを盛った汁物）（　④　）

焼物（yakimono—焼き魚）（　⑤　）

蒸物（mushimono—蒸した野菜・魚介類）（　⑥　）

飯・味噌汁・香の物（meshi・misoshiru・konomono）（　⑦　）

Notes ＊ 寸は長さの単位。1寸は約3.03cm。よって料理が盛られる皿の大きさは約24×24cm。

A　steamed vegetables, seafood, etc.

B　sliced raw fish or vegetables in vinegar

C　boiled fish or meat with vegetables and other ingredients in a clear soup

D　hors d'oeuvres

E　grilled fish

F　rice, soybean paste soup, pickles

G　various delicacies on a large square tray

Part **2** Telephone Communication

SCENE

共同プロジェクト会議が無事に終わり帰途につく前に、Eco
Motors社のTom Davis取締役はElec International社の谷明
社長に電話をかけています。ここでは、**「感謝を述べるときの
コミュニケーション」**のしかたがポイントとなります。

1 ▶ Listening（1）

Davis取締役と谷社長のダイアログを聞いて、次の各文の内容が正しければTを、間違っていればFを選びなさい。

1   Mr. Davis wants to see Mr. Tani before he returns to the U.S.   T / F
2   Mr. Tani hopes to cultivate a relationship with Eco Motors.   T / F
3   Mr. Davis had a pleasant stay in Japan.   T / F

2 ▶ Listening（2）

もう一度ダイアログを聞きながら空欄を埋めなさい。ダイアログが完成したらリピート練習をしなさい。

Mr. Davis: Hello. This is Tom Davis. Could I talk to Mr. Tani, please?

Secretary: Just a second, please. ①_____.

Mr. Tani: Hello, Tom. How can I help you?

Mr. Davis: I just wanted to ②_____.(*1) We appreciate your
　　　　　③_____ during our stay.

Mr. Tani: Oh, you are most welcome. I'm glad we've had a successful session.
　　　　　I ④_____ the project.

Mr. Davis: Yes, we're looking forward to ⑤_____ on this project.

Mr. Tani: Yes, we will do our best to ⑥_____ (*2) and hope our good
　　　　　relationship will ⑦_____.

Mr. Davis: OK, then, thank you for everything again.

Mr. Tani: Have a good flight back home.

Mr. Davis: Thank you. See you.

Mr. Tani: Bye.

Notes *1 「感謝する」の表現。express one's appreciationなども使える。
　　　　*2 「～の期待にそう」の表現。live up to one's expectationsなども使える。

3 ▶ Role Play

完成したダイアログを使ってロールプレイ練習をしなさい。

4 ▶ Conversation Map

それぞれの英語のせりふを考えて、電話でのコミュニケーションを成立させなさい。完成したらペアで会話しなさい。

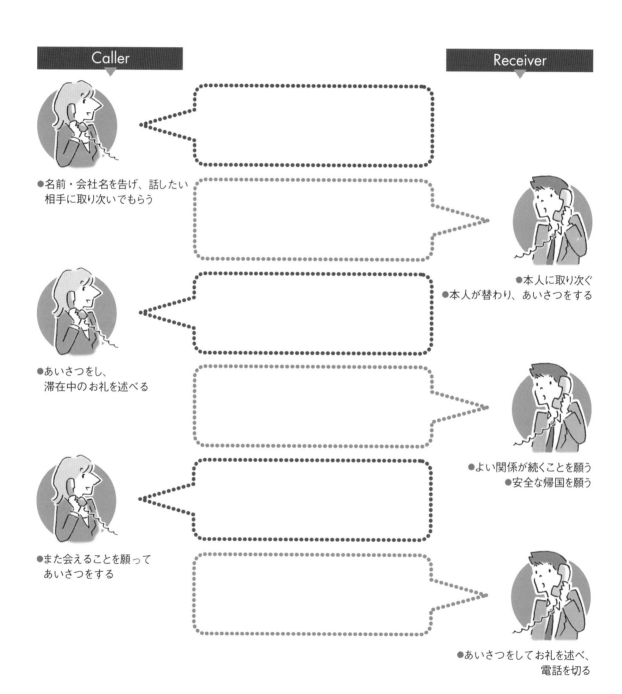

Caller

Receiver

●名前・会社名を告げ、話したい
　相手に取り次いでもらう

●本人に取り次ぐ
●本人が替わり、あいさつをする

●あいさつをし、
　滞在中のお礼を述べる

●よい関係が続くことを願う
●安全な帰国を願う

●また会えることを願って
　あいさつをする

●あいさつをしてお礼を述べ、
　電話を切る

Business Topic ▶ ⓬

海外のビジネスパートナーを接待する

1 次の英文から、「海外のビジネスパートナーを接待する際の留意点」を読み取りなさい。

2 音声を聞きながらシャドーイングの練習をしなさい。

Entertaining Overseas Business Partners

Inviting business associates to dinner is a valuable opportunity to deepen the relationship with them. When it comes to overseas counterparts, there are cases where they may adhere to dietary restrictions based on religion, personal eating habits, allergies, etc. Accordingly, dinner hosts should become familiar with such preferences. One example is vegetarians, who are broadly classified as vegetarian or vegan. Vegans are full vegetarians, and vegetarians are those with slightly fewer restrictions than vegans. Some vegetarians eat fish, eggs and dairy products. In this connection, for religious reasons, Muslims do not eat pork. Some Muslim denominations[*1] do not even eat mollusks[*2] such as squid, or crustaceans[*3] such as lobster. Furthermore, drinking is considered taboo, although this varies by country. In principle, Muslims prefer "Halal food"[*4] that is religiously certified.

*1 宗派 　*2 軟体動物 　*3 甲殻類動物
*4 ハラル・フードとは、イスラム法上許された食べ物のこと。近年では食べ物だけでなく化粧品や化粧道具、飲食店などの施設などにもハラル認証が適用されている。

Business Tips

世界の宗教人口

世界の宗教別人口は現在キリスト教徒が最多で、2070年にはイスラム教徒とキリスト教徒がほぼ同数になり、2100年になるとイスラム教徒が最多になると予測されています。2010年のキリスト教徒は約21億7千万人、イスラム教徒は約16億人で、それぞれ世界人口の31.4%と23.2%を占めています。国別のイスラム教徒数については、インドネシア（2億人）、インド（1億7000万人）、パキスタン（1億6000万人）、バングラデシュ（1億3000万人）、ナイジェリア（7700万人）、エジプト（7700万人）、イラン（7400万人）、トルコ（7100万人）、サウジアラビア（2600万人）です。

（出典）米調査機関ピュー・リサーチ・センター

実践ビジネス英語

検印
省略

2011 年 1 月 20 日　第 1 版発行
2015 年 1 月 30 日　第 5 刷発行
©2020 年 1 月 31 日　第 2 版第 1 刷発行
2023 年 1 月 31 日　第 3 刷発行

編著者　　　　　　　　辻　　和　　成
　　　　　　　　　　　辻　　勢　　都
　　　　　　　　　　　Margaret M. Lieb

発行者　　　　　　　　原　　雅　　久
発行所　　　　　　株式会社 朝日出版社
　　　　〒101-0065 東京都千代田区西神田 3-3-5
　　　　　　電話　東京　(03) 3239-0271
　　　　　　FAX　東京　(03) 3239-0479
　　　　　E-mail　text-e@asahipress.com
　　　　　　振替口座　00140-2-46008
　　　　　　https://www.asahipress.com/
　　　　組版／メディアアート　製版／錦明印刷

ISBN 978-4-255-15659-0